365

S0-FQL-785

Motivational
Thoughts
for Women

© 2006 by Barbour Publishing, Inc.

ISBN 1-59789-208-4

Text is taken from *Today! Motivational Thoughts for Women* by
Nancy Walker Hale, published by Barbour Publishing, Inc.

All rights reserved. No part of this publication may be reproduced or transmitted
for commercial purposes, except for brief quotations in printed reviews, without
written permission of the publisher.

Published by Barbour Publishing, Inc., P.O. Box 719, Uhrichsville, Ohio 44683
www.barbourbooks.com

*Our mission is to publish and distribute inspirational products offering
exceptional value and biblical encouragement to the masses.*

Member of the
Evangelical Christian
Publishers Association

Printed in Thailand
5 4 3 2

Today!
I will face the person in the
mirror with enthusiasm.

365

Motivational Thoughts for Women

Nancy Walker Hale

BARBOUR
PUBLISHING

December 30

Today!
I will clip a newspaper article about
someone I know and mail it to her
with a congratulatory note.

Today!
I will join a widowed person
in the church pew.

Today!
I will forget my troubles
and put on a smile.

December 28

Today!
I will volunteer to help
in the church nursery.

Today!
I will do something uplifting
for someone less fortunate.

Today!
I will refuse to let malice enter my mind.

January 3

Today!
I will direct my thoughts
toward others, not myself.

Today!
I will hate unholiness.

Today!
I will listen more than I talk.

Today!
I will celebrate the true
reason for the season.

January 5

Today!
I will refrain from criticizing others.

December 24

Today!
I will begin to better myself.

Today!
I will take a break from
the stresses of life.

Today!
I will let someone else get
the credit for my work.

January 7

Today!
I will let someone know how
much I love them.

Today!
I will overlook a slight, intentional or not.

January 8

Today!
I will do something fun with a child.

December 21

Today!
I will clean a messy area of my house.

January 9

Today!
I will give to a worthwhile charity.

December 20

Today!
I will persevere, persevere, persevere.

Today!
I will reconnect with an old friend.

December 19

Today!
I will create a happy moment
for myself or for others.

Today!
I will pamper myself.

Today!
I will dissolve misunderstandings.

Today!
I will eliminate waste in one area of my life.

December 17

Today!
I will confess my sins of omission.

Today!
I will think before speaking.

December 16

Today!
I will confess my sins of commission.

January 14

Today!
I will end gossip when it reaches me.

December 15

Today!
I will tread gently on
other's fragile emotions.

January 15

Today!
I will take the first step
in restoring a relationship.

December 14

Today!
I will snub no one.

Today!
I will clean up after myself.

Today!
I will acquaint myself with all of
my closest neighbors.

January 17

Today!
I will pat someone else on the back.

December 12

Today!
I will adapt my behavior to
suit each circumstance.

January 18

Today!
I will spend time with an elderly person.

December 11

Today!
I will expect the best to happen,
not imagine the worst.

Today!
I will compliment someone
on a job well done.

December 10

Today!
I will cover my day with prayer.

January 20

Today!
I will enjoy sight.

December 9

Today!
I will yield to the temptation of
doing an anonymous good deed.

January 21

Today!
I will push away the plate
before second or third helpings.

Today!
I will brush any chips off my
shoulder before they fall and mash
my (or someone else's) toes.

January 22

Today!
I will not be so straightlaced.

Today!
I will turn my best intention into
an even better deed.

January 23

Today!
I will put my troubles and work
aside and read a good book.

Today!
I will have Christ-confidence that will
bolster me from the invasion of inferiority.

January 24

Today!
I will set an attainable goal.

Today!
I will allow humility to shield me from
the hailstones of superiority.

January 25

Today!
I will reach a previously set goal.

December 4

Today!
I will stamp out the irritating
bugs within my personality.

January 26

Today!
I will celebrate life!

December 3

Today!
I will shut the door on the disgusting
habits that try to enter my life.

January 27

Today!
I will be kind to animals.

December 2

Today!

I will have contentment walk beside me.

January 28

Today!
I will donate a few hours of my time to a
worthwhile community activity.

Today!
I will shelter an abused person, if
not physically, then with prayer.

Today!
I will change my routine.

November 30

Today!
I will open my home with
warm hospitality to others.

Today!
I will eat healthy meals.

Today!
I will not let discouragement creep in
like a heavy fog obscuring my vision.

Today!
I will worship God.

Today!
I will concentrate on the
pluses, not the minuses.

Today!
I will pay homage to an ancestor.

Today!
I will be a friend to the friendless.

Today!
I will surprise someone pleasantly.

Today!
I will do it right the first time.

Today!
I will tell my parents how much I
appreciate their sacrifices for me.

Today!
I will stitch up small tears in relationships
before they become major ones.

Today!
I will relinquish a grudge.

Today!
I will obey God's laws.

Today!
I will congratulate someone
else on her success.

Today!
I will erase the memory of, but not
the lessons from, my past errors.

February 6

Today!
I will exercise a part of my
body other than my tongue.

Today!
I will make a list of things
for which I am thankful.

February 7

Today!
I will greet others with a smile.

Today!
I will listen to quality music.

February 8

Today!
I won't worry about tomorrow.

Today!
I will wear a pleasant look on my face.

Today!
I will change my
"should have dones" to "dids."

November 19

Today!
I will back up my convictions
with appropriate actions.

Today!
I will give 110 percent to the task at hand.

November 18

Today!
I will reinforce good behavior
in myself and in others.

February 11

Today!
I will visit a sick friend.

November 17

Today!
I will toss away unhealthy
coping methods in my life.

February 12

Today!
I will be a person of integrity.

Today!
I will consider tomorrow in view of the
consequences of today's moments.

February 13

Today!
I will dismiss anger before it festers.

Today!
I will perform at an optimum
level in whatever I do.

Today!
I will show gratitude for any act of
kindness toward me.

Today!
I will strive to reach the potential that
God had in mind when He created me.

Today!
I will force myself to be
as active as possible.

November 13

Today!
I will muster enough
resources to be energetic.

February 16

Today!

I will not impose on friends.

Today!
I will harbor fresh goodwill toward
others instead of aging grudges.

Today!
I will wisely plan a future event.

November 11

Today!
I will remember a veteran.

Today!
I will pray for peace within my home.

Today!
I will believe that God will give
me the desires of my heart.

February 19

Today!
I will be patient while waiting.

Today!
I will wash my hands of
anything reeking of deceit.

Today!
I will share something with another person.

Today!
I will give my undivided attention
when someone speaks to me.

Today!
I will take the first step in
conquering my fear.

Today!
I will awaken with a thankful heart.

Today!

I will not be a doormat for others.

Today!
I will return a borrowed
item—with interest.

Today!
I will give others enough personal space.

Today!
I will maintain the proper
balance in my life.

February 24

Today!
I will listen to another's opinion
without arguing or criticizing.

Today!
I will deplete the envy reservoir in my life.

Today!
I will pray for peace within
my neighborhood.

Today!
I will begin to build a support system to
help me through the valleys of my life.

February 26

Today!
I will pray for peace within my country.

Today!
I will make a list and complete three
of the most important things on it.

February 27

Today!
I will pray for world peace.

November 1

Today!
I will increase my vitality by
decreasing my stress.

February 28

Today!
I will keep myself morally straight.

Today!
I will be a proper steward of all
that God has entrusted to me.

March 1

Today!
I will read my Bible.

Today!
I will be a better money manager.

March 2

Today!
I will set a good example for others
who may be watching my actions.

Today!
I will clear my thoughts of any
plots to "get even."

March 3

Today!
I will take time to listen to the birds sing.

October 28

Today!
I will memorize scripture.

Today!
I will lead with authority.

October 27

Today!
I will make compassion my creed.

March 5

Today!
I will plant a flower or a tree.

Today!
I will have moderation as my motto.

March 6

Today!
I will block out unpleasant memories.

Today!
I will not let others intimidate me.

Today!
I will find something to laugh about.

Today!
I will spend the day as
though it were my last.

March 8

Today!
I will scrub something until it sparkles.

Today!
I will listen to my own heart's desires.

March 9

Today!
I will concentrate on purity.

Today!
I will be pleasant to live with.

March 10

Today!
I will show respect for
another's belongings.

Today!
I will shield my mind from coveting
others' wealth, status, or beauty.

March 11

Today!
I will show appreciation to
an authority figure.

Today!
I will guard the door of my
heart from Satan's attacks.

March 12

Today!
I will be a mentor.

Today!
I will carry someone else's burden.

Today!
I will be thankful for the things
I can do without pain.

Today!
I will do a good deed in secret.

March 14

Today!
I will support clean living by example.

Today!
I will forget past slights against me.

March 15

Today!
I will set appropriate priorities
regarding my time.

Today!
I will practice mercy.

March 16

Today!
I will read something to
broaden my knowledge.

Today!
I will meditate on past
deliverance from troubles.

March 17

Today!
I will get out in the fresh air instead
of staying cooped up inside.

October 14

Today!
I will muzzle my mouth when
volcanic acid threatens to spew.

March 18

Today!
I will leave a good tip for
excellent services rendered.

Today!
I will leave my heavy bag
of false guilt with Jesus.

March 19

Today!
I will put others before myself.

Today!
I will leave vengeance in
the Lord's hands.

March 20

Today!
I will spend some time alone to
recharge my emotional batteries.

Today!
I will refuse to accept for myself
any honor belonging to God.

March 21

Today!
I will spend some time with God to
recharge my spiritual batteries.

Today!
I will let Jesus collect five minutes' worth
of my tears and twenty-three hours and
fifty-five minutes of my praise.

Today!
I will recommit myself to a predetermined,
but almost forgotten, purpose.

Today!
I will nip a budding sin before
it blooms into a prickly cactus.

March 23

Today!
I will save for something special
instead of buying on credit.

October 8

Today!
I will overcome timidity and
speak up for righteousness.

March 24

Today!
I will learn something new.

Today!
I will deny the urge to burst
someone's bubble.

March 25

Today!
I will be a friend in deed.

Today!
I will pretend that my
problems don't exist.

March 26

Today!
I will teach something helpful to someone.

Today!
I will offer to relieve someone who is
sitting with a bedridden family member.

March 27

Today!
I will forgive myself.

October 4

Today!
I will ask a children's home what
it needs and provide it, even if it
is just a pack of pencils.

March 28

Today!
I will recycle.

Today!
I will give some time that I can't really
spare to lend a listening ear to a needy soul.

March 29

Today!
I will be gentle.

Today!
I will spread good news,
not the opposite.

March 30

Today!
I will count my blessings.

October 1

Today!
I will live God's way.

Today!
I will live in the present, not the past.

Today!
I will make humor a part of my routine.

April 1

Today!
I will listen to good music.

September 29

Today!
I will accept my past.

April 2

Today!
I will relax.

Today!
I will make injustice my adversary.

Today!
I will put first things first.

Today!
I will chase away unwholesome thoughts.

April 4

Today!
I will reflect on how I might
spend the rest of my life.

Today!
I will use my minutes wisely since they
disappear as rapidly as snowflakes melt.

April 5

Today!
I will be less critical of others around me.

September 25

Today!
I will recognize unwanted interruptions as
opportunities for ministry rather
than reasons for frustration.

April 6

Today!
I will do a good deed for another
without expecting compensation.

Today!
I will choose to be joyful.

April 7

Today!
I will be thankful for what I have.

Today!
I will not allow the warped values of the
world to invade my personal convictions.

April 8

Today!
I will become involved in
something worthy of my time
and needy of my talents.

Today!
I will let discretion be my ally.

Today!
I will reminisce about the good times in my
life, rather than dwelling on the bad times.

Today!
I will disinfect myself of my own faults
before dissecting those of others.

April 10

Today!
I will spend more time in prayer for
others than for me and mine.

September 20

Today!
I will mean what I say, and
say what I mean.

April 11

Today!
I will take action.

Today!
I will savor each moment of glory as if
it were a cup of water to parched lips.

Today!
I will eliminate a "want" in
order to meet a "need."

September 18

Today!
I will be an advocate for someone
too weak to speak for himself.

April 13

Today!
I will be kind to all of God's creation.

September 17

Today!
I will plant the seed of hope in
someone whose garden of life is
currently full of weeds.

April 14

Today!
I will direct my thoughts toward gratitude.

Today!
I will enjoy life's spontaneity.

April 15

Today!
I will have my outlook
be upward, not inward.

Today!
I will say no to a request that someone else
should do if I am already overextended.

April 16

Today!
I will "be," not "do."

September 14

Today!
I will spend more time on my knees in
prayer than I did yesterday.

April 17

Today!
I will volunteer my money and time for
a greater cause than my desires.

Today!
I will do my best, no matter
what I attempt to do.

April 18

Today!
I will be satisfied.

September 12

Today!
I will ask God to give me a job to
do for Him, and then I'll do it.

April 19

Today!
I will make the effort to smile
whether I feel like it or not.

September 11

Today!
I will let someone go ahead of me in the
checkout line, especially if they have
two items and I have twenty-two.

April 20

Today!
I will serve God.

September 10

Today!
I will set my standards a little
higher than before.

April 21

Today!
I will be honest.

September 9

Today!
I will hush evil thoughts as they
attempt to enter my mind.

April 22

Today!
I will be hopeful concerning the future.

Today!
I will rest my weary bones before they
shout too loudly that I've waited too long.

Today!
I will rejoice in the day that
the Lord has made.

Today!
I will count my blessings instead of
rehashing my burdens.

Today!
I will patiently endure my
current circumstances.

Today!

I will keep an eye on quality, not quantity.

April 25

Today!
I will continue to work to reach a
goal in spite of opposition,
ridicule, and interruptions.

September 5

Today!
I will live a life pleasing to God.

Today!
I will seek to know God better.

September 4

Today!
I will be a breath of fresh,
rather than foul, air.

April 27

Today!
I will try to be more Christlike in
my actions and speech.

Today!
I will avoid impropriety.

April 28

Today!
I will begin a new habit to
improve my health.

September 2

Today!
I will donate books currently collecting
dust to a worthwhile book sale.

April 29

Today!
I will be a cheerful giver.

Today!
I will contribute to the Scouts
or any other organizations training
youth to be prepared (not just
for campouts, but for life).

Today!
I will sing with my heart, if
not with my voice.

August 31

Today!
I will bring extra to a potluck supper.

Today!
I will give to God what
belongs to God (tithe!).

August 30

Today!
I will be a sermon in shoes—I may be the
only "Bible" some people read.

Today!
I will complete a necessary
task, no matter how unpleasant.

Today!
I will be thrifty, but not stingy.

May 3

Today!
I will celebrate even the smallest victory
to encourage others or myself.

Today!
I will remember to record a momentous
occasion with a camcorder or camera.

May 4

Today!
I will be slow to become angry.

August 27

Today!
I will send a "Thinking of You" card
to an acquaintance who's out of sight,
but not out of mind.

May 5

Today!
I will be fair.

August 26

Today!
I will say grace in a restaurant.

May 6

Today!
I will persevere, even if
the going gets rough.

Today!
I will realize that discipline must
accompany desire to achieve results.

May 7

Today!
I will be determined to do what is right.

August 24

Today!
I will recycle magazines by giving them to
a hospital, nursing home, doctor's office,
dentist's office, or hairdresser.

Today!

I will be an overcomer.

August 23

Today!
I will bake some cookies for
a homebound person.

May 9

Today!
I will not hesitate when I see an
opportunity to help another.

Today!
I will baby-sit for a young couple desperate
for an evening (or weekend) away from the
draining demands of parenthood.

May 10

Today!
I will refrain from bragging.

August 21

Today!
I will escape from the whirlwind of the
daily grind with a cup of hot tea.

May 11

Today!
I will show appreciation for a teacher.

August 20

Today!
I will refuse to force myself into a
lane of traffic that might place
others or me in jeopardy.

May 12

Today!
I will be creative.

August 19

Today!
I will tell my child (parent, spouse, friend, relative, neighbor, dog) that I love them.

May 13

Today!
I will be an encourager.

August 18

Today!
I will share the joy of answered prayer.

May 14

Today!
I will be a friend.

August 17

Today!
I will pray for the country's politicians
during governmental chaos.

May 15

Today!
I will be supportive.

Today!
I will lean on God's strength, not my own.

May 16

Today!
I will be free from fears.

August 15

Today!
I will do the most important things first.

May 17

Today!
I will be alert to perceive
the needs of others.

August 14

Today!
I will apologize for acting out of
character during a moment of stress.

May 18

Today!
I will be enthusiastic about life.

Today!
I will get rid of anything I
haven't worn in two years.

May 19

Today!
I will be a stimulating conversationalist.

August 12

Today!
I will update all my
personal correspondence.

May 20

Today!
I will be interesting and interested
in what others have to say.

August 11

Today!
I will simplify my life by
decreasing my debt.

May 21

Today!
I will be warm and friendly
to those I meet.

August 10

Today!
I will pray for the end of terrorism.

May 22

Today!
I will keep a secret when asked to do so.

Today!
I will pray for the world's
economic situation.

May 23

Today!
I will avoid procrastination.

August 8

Today!
I will clip a newspaper article of interest to someone I know and mail it to her.

Today!
I will avoid making mountains
out of molehills.

Today!
I will visit a nursing home and
hug an older person.

May 25

Today!
I will have peace reign in my life.

August 6

Today!
I will seek the good in people.

May 26

Today!
I will have joy rule in my household.

Today!
I will give a peace offering.

May 27

Today!
I will do the work that is required of me
and not be concerned if others seem to
have more by doing less.

August 4

Today!
I will smile anyway.

May 28

Today!
I will be shrewd but innocent.

Today!
I will schedule that doctor's appointment
I've been putting off.

May 29

Today!
I will not put myself in a prison
of my own making and limit
what I should be doing.

August 2

Today!
I will donate a box of books to
a library or school.

Today!

I will heed a wiser person's advice.

August 1

Today!
I will keep moving although my
body feels as if it's full of lead.

May 31

Today!
I will value my freedoms.

July 31

Today!
I will take a carload of items
to the Salvation Army or
other charitable institution.

June 1

Today!
I will rest and restore my soul.

July 30

Today!
I will do something that I enjoy doing
along with the things I have to do.

Today!
I will improve my home in some way.

July 29

Today!
I will fill my mind with positive thoughts of
the future, not negatives from the past.

Today!
I will strengthen a relationship.

Today!
I will praise a child for an
accomplishment—big or small.

June 4

Today!
I will ponder God's perfect
will for my life.

July 27

Today!
I will celebrate someone's
contribution to the world.

June 5

Today!
I will stifle my greed.

July 26

Today!
I will watch a "decent" movie
uncluttered with violence,
graphic sex scenes, or profanity.

Today!
I will be a willing helper.

Today!
I will read a book that will
challenge my thinking.

June 7

Today!
I will be a good neighbor, regardless of
what kind of neighbor I have.

July 24

Today!
I will do a task correctly, or not at all.

Today!
I will brighten someone's day.

July 23

Today!
I will organize all the photographs
strewn around my house.

Today!
I will meet someone's need.

July 22

Today!
I will double-check my work to
make sure it was done correctly.

June 10

Today!
I will not give up.

Today!
I will call someone who lives alone.

Today!
I will believe that help is
just around the corner.

Today!
I will acquiesce to
someone else's decision.

Today!
I will not yield to
temptation to do wrong.

July 19

Today!
I will have faith that everything
will turn out okay.

June 13

Today!
I will help someone going
through a difficult time.

July 18

Today!
I will act as if I am courageous.

Today!
I will keep the end result in mind.

July 17

Today!
I will take a risk.

June 15

Today!
I will be quick to give
sincere compliments.

Today!
I will make my emotional
skin elephant-hide thick.

June 16

Today!
I will refuse to make someone else
miserable just because I am.

July 15

Today!
I will have my desires be compatible
with God's desires for me.

June 17

Today!
I will not harbor a grudge.

July 14

Today!
I will keep my head when all
those around me do not.

June 18

Today!
I will trust that my heartache will
eventually turn to joy.

Today!
I will set boundaries to protect
me from destruction.

June 19

Today!
I will have confidence in myself.

July 12

Today!
I will be the first to take the initiative in standing up for righteousness.

June 20

Today!
I will treat others with respect
to maintain my own self-respect.

July 11

Today!
I will expand my horizons by
doing something totally foreign
to my past experiences.

June 21

Today!
I will not nag.

July 10

Today!
I will let Christ's example, not peer
expectations, determine my decisions.

June 22

Today!
I will not say, "I told you so."

Today!
I will make Christ my role model.

June 23

Today!
I will do something out
of my comfort zone.

July 8

Today!
I will not allow temporary frustrations
and disappointments to
permanently alter my goals.

June 24

Today!
I will make my aches and
pains invisible to others.

Today!
I will be an exemplary role model
for those around me.

June 25

Today!
I will allow silence to be golden.

July 6

Today!
I will have the courage to be the light that
exposes the darkness of wrongdoing.

Today!
I will make clutter disappear
from my desk.

July 5

Today!
I will send a note of appreciation to
someone who might least expect it.

June 27

Today!
I will not leave the gas tank
on empty for the next driver.

July 4

Today!
I will plan an event to occur in the
very near future, to give me
something to look forward to.

June 28

Today!
I will challenge my mind.

Today!
I will make recharging my
"batteries" a priority.

Today!
I will not repeat yesterday's mistakes.

July 2

Today!
I will make music appreciation
a part of my routine.

Today!
I will stretch my limits.

July 1

Today!
I will not allow garbage into my mind.

BLESS YOUR HEART

Heartland Samplers, Inc.
9947 Valley View Road
Eden Prairie, MN 55344

T4-ABK-305

BLESS YOUR HEART

Heartland Samplers, Inc.
Copyright © 1987

The Scripture quotations are from the following sources:
NEW AMERICAN STANDARD BIBLE (NASB) © 1977 by
The Lockman Foundation. Used by permission. Scripture
quotations marked NIV are from the Holy Bible, NEW
INTERNATIONAL VERSION. Copyright © 1973, 1978,
1984 International Bible Society. Used by permission of
Zondervan Bible Publishers. Scripture quotations from the
GOOD NEWS BIBLE, the Bible in Today's English Version
(GNB) Copyright American Bible Society 1966, 1971,
1976 used by permission. Verses marked TLB are taken
from THE LIVING BIBLE, Copyright 1971 by Tyndale
House Publishers, Wheaton, IL. Used by permission.
Hymns marked * were used by permission from Covenant
Press, Chicago, IL.
All rights reserved including the right to reproduce this
book or portions therof in any form.
10 9 8 7

I find that doing the will of God leaves me no time for disputing about His plans.

Macdonald

I know the plans I have for you, declares the Lord, plans to prosper and not to harm you, plans to give you hope and a future.

Jer. 29:11 NIV

JANUARY 11

Sometimes you can make a more effective statement by holding your tongue.

Lord, help me to submit my feelings and my tongue to Your control so that they won't control me. Amen.

JULY 12

Timely good deeds are nicer than afterthoughts. The smallest good deed is better than the grandest intention.

Almighty and merciful God, may I cheerfully accomplish those things which you would have me do this day. Amen.

 **JANUARY 12**

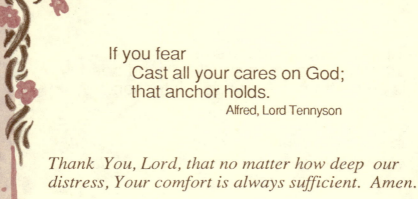

If you fear
    Cast all your cares on God;
    that anchor holds.

Alfred, Lord Tennyson

Thank You, Lord, that no matter how deep our distress, Your comfort is always sufficient. Amen.

JULY 13

Another year is dawning
Dear Father, let it be,
In working or in waiting,
Another year with thee.

F. R. Havergol

Seek ye first His kingdom and His
righteousness, and all these things
will be added unto you.

Matt. 6:33 KJV

JANUARY 1

Obey me and I will be your God and you shall be my people; only do as I say and all shall be well.

Jer. 7:23 TLB

Lord God, how we as a people, as a country, need You. Change our hearts and give us the desire to obey You. Amen.

JULY 2

If we fill our hours with regrets of yesterday and with the worries of tomorrow, we have no today in which to be thankful.

Father, help me to see the beauty of today and to be thankful for what You have provided. Amen.

 JANUARY 2

Whatever America hopes to bring to pass in the world must first come to pass in the heart of America.

Dwight D. Eisenhower

Lord, begin with my heart. Amen.

JULY 3

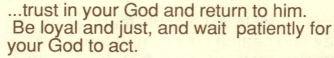

...trust in your God and return to him. Be loyal and just, and wait patiently for your God to act.

Hos. 12:6 GNB

Father, help me to take the time during these days in January to sit quietly and to wait before Thee. Amen.

JANUARY 3

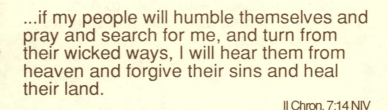

...if my people will humble themselves and pray and search for me, and turn from their wicked ways, I will hear them from heaven and forgive their sins and heal their land.

II Chron. 7:14 NIV

God bless America...

JULY 4

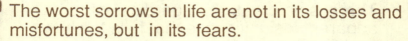

The worst sorrows in life are not in its losses and misfortunes, but in its fears.

A.C. Benson

God, our Father, fill me with a continual sense of Your presence, dispelling all my fears with Your peace. Amen.

JANUARY 4

There is no creature, regardless of its apparent insignificance that fails to show us something of God's goodness.

T. a Kempis

Thank You Father, for Your goodness that I see everywhere. Help me to remember that no one is insignificant in Your sight. Amen.

JULY 5

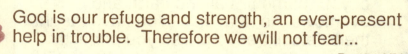

God is our refuge and strength, an ever-present
help in trouble. Therefore we will not fear...

Ps. 46:1 NIV

"Be still, and know that I am God..."

Ps. 46:10 NIV

 **JANUARY 5**

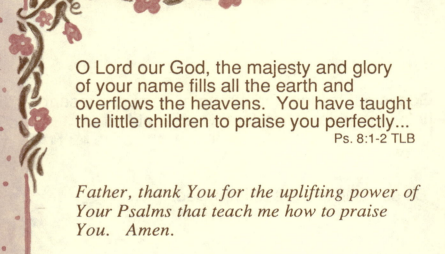

O Lord our God, the majesty and glory
of your name fills all the earth and
overflows the heavens. You have taught
the little children to praise you perfectly...

Ps. 8:1-2 TLB

*Father, thank You for the uplifting power of
Your Psalms that teach me how to praise
You. Amen.*

JULY 6

Prayer is the mortar that holds our house together.

Mother Theresa

There had never been such a day before, and there has never been another since, when the Lord stopped the sun and moon - all because of the prayer of one man!

Joshua 10:14 TLB

JANUARY 13

...when the Holy Spirit controls our lives he
will produce this kind of fruit in us -
love
joy
peace
patience
kindness
goodness
faithfulness
gentleness
self-control...

Gal. 5:22 TLB

JULY 14

Home is not given, but made.

Father, light up the small duties of this day. May they shine with the beauty of Your presence. May I find glory in the small common task before me. Amen.

JANUARY 6

Everything has its beauty
but not everyone sees it.

Lord, give me eyes to see deeper than the surface.
Amen.

JULY 7

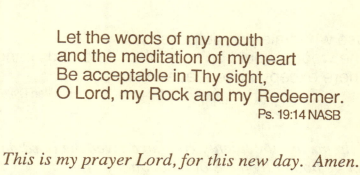

Let the words of my mouth
and the meditation of my heart
Be acceptable in Thy sight,
O Lord, my Rock and my Redeemer.

Ps. 19:14 NASB

This is my prayer Lord, for this new day. Amen.

JANUARY 7

Use what talents you possess;
the woods would be very silent if no birds sang
there except those that sang best.

Henry Van Dyke

Help me use the talents You have given me Lord and not be bound by fears of inadequacy. Amen.

JULY 8

I give You thanks, O Lord, for the uniqueness in each snowflake - just like the uniqueness in each of us.

Lord, may I look for the special qualities that are present in each person that I meet today and may I give You the thanks for them. Amen.

JANUARY 8

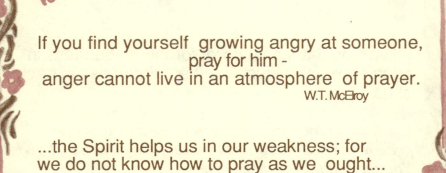

If you find yourself growing angry at someone,
pray for him -
anger cannot live in an atmosphere of prayer.

W.T. McElroy

...the Spirit helps us in our weakness; for
we do not know how to pray as we ought...

Rom. 8:26 RSV

JULY 9

We would be well on the way to perfection if we could weed out one vice from ourselves each year.

T. á Kempis

"Search me, O God, and know my heart; test me and know my anxious thoughts."

Ps. 139:23 NIV

Father, give me the desire to follow through on what You show me.   Amen.

JANUARY 9

We Christians have no veil over our faces; we can be mirrors that brightly reflect the glory of the Lord. And as the Spirit of the Lord works within us, we become more and more like him.

II Cor. 3:18 TLB

Lord, help me break through the facade and see myself more clearly. I want to reflect Your glory. Amen.

JULY 10

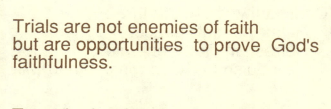

Trials are not enemies of faith
but are opportunities to prove God's
faithfulness.

Trust the Lord and sincerely worship him;
think of all the tremendous things he has
done for you.

I Sam. 12:24 TLB

JANUARY 10

In Christianity, there are three **R**'s:
   Relax in God's peace,
   Refresh in God's energies,
   Relinquish to God's wisdom and will.

There is much out of order in my life Lord. I give it all to You and ask You to take all the fragments and remake them into a new whole. Amen.

JULY 11

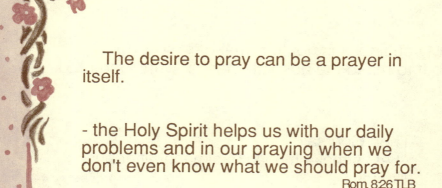

The desire to pray can be a prayer in itself.

- the Holy Spirit helps us with our daily problems and in our praying when we don't even know what we should pray for.

Rom. 8:26 TLB

JANUARY 14

My business is not to remake myself,
but to make the absolute best of what God made.

Robert Browning

Then God said,
"Let us make man in our image, after our
likeness..."

Gen. 1:26 RSV

 JULY 15

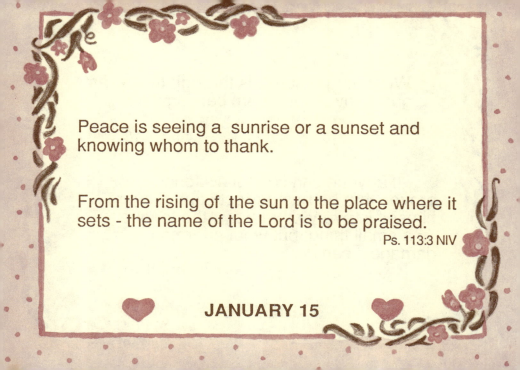

Peace is seeing a sunrise or a sunset and knowing whom to thank.

From the rising of the sun to the place where it sets - the name of the Lord is to be praised.

Ps. 113:3 NIV

JANUARY 15

When anger spreads through the breast,
guard thy tongue from barking idly.

Sappho

If anyone can control his tongue, it
proves that he has perfect control over
himself in every other way...the tongue
is a small thing, but what enormous
damage it can do...

James 3:2,5 TLB

JULY 16

Prayer is neither black magic nor is it a form of demand note. Prayer is a relationship.

John Heuss

Lord, when I pray, also make me aware of listening to what You might have to say to me. Amen.

JANUARY 16

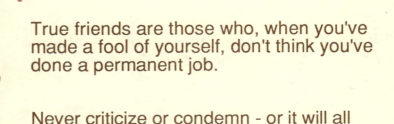

True friends are those who, when you've made a fool of yourself, don't think you've done a permanent job.

Never criticize or condemn - or it will all come back on you. Go easy on others; then they will do the same for you.

Luke 6:37 TLB

JULY 17

Be gentle and ready to forgive; never hold grudges. Remember, the Lord forgave you, so you must forgive others.

Col. 3:13 TLB

I need to be reminded so often Lord. Amen.

JANUARY 17

Bless the Lord, O my soul; and all that is within me, bless his holy name.

Ps. 103:1 NASB

Creator and lover of beauty, I adore You for the splendor of the earth. Amen.

JULY 18

Do more than exist ...   live
                    touch ...   feel
                    look ...   observe
                    read ...   absorb
                    hear ...   listen...

Lord, help me to live in a way pleasing to You - loving others and fulfilling my potential. Amen.

JANUARY 18

Sunday is the golden clasp that binds together the volume of the week.

Longfellow

Remember the Sabbath to keep it holy.

Ex. 20:8 RSV

JULY 19

Life is like a game of tennis; the player who serves well seldom loses.

Lord, I give You my hands and my heart - make my heart willing and my hands ready to do Your will. Amen.

 JANUARY 19

Thou dost rule the swelling of the sea;
When its waves rise,
Thou dost still them.

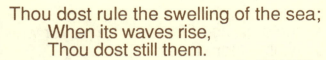

Ps. 89:9 NASB

Sometimes I fear the waves will sweep over me, Lord. Thank You for the assurance that You are in control. I put my trust in You. Amen.

JULY 20

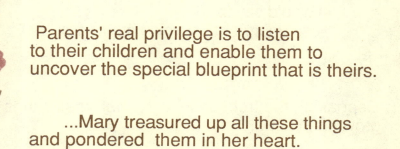

Parents' real privilege is to listen
to their children and enable them to
uncover the special blueprint that is theirs.

...Mary treasured up all these things
and pondered them in her heart.

Luke 2:1 NIV

JANUARY 20

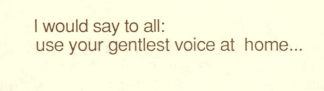

I would say to all:
use your gentlest voice at home...

...speaking the truth in love, we will in all things
grow up in him...

Eph. 4:15 NIV

JULY 21

Each man can interpret another's experience only by his own.

Thoreau

Encourage one another and build each other up, just as in fact you are doing.

I Thes. 5:11 NIV

 **JANUARY 21**

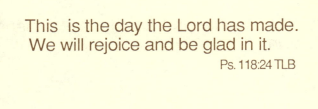

This is the day the Lord has made.
We will rejoice and be glad in it.

Ps. 118:24 TLB

Father, I thank You for keeping me safe through last night and for the beginning of another day. Amen.

JULY 22

Quietly trust yourself to Christ your Lord
and if anybody asks why you believe
as you do, be ready to tell him, and do it in
a gentle and respectful way.

I Peter 3:15 TLB

Lord, at times I find it so difficult to
communicate Your love to others.
I hold back, afraid to acknowledge You.
Help me to speak freely to others of what is
most precious to me. Amen.

JANUARY 22

Glowing moments of peaceful reflection kindle the growth of our minds and spirits.

Father, help me to set aside some time today to sit quietly and listen to Your creation. Center my thoughts on Your loving kindness and goodness to me. Amen.

JULY 23

Just as there comes a warm sunbeam into every cottage window,
so comes a love - born of God's care for every separate need.

Nathaniel Hawthorne

The very hairs of your head are numbered.

Matt. 10:30 NIV

JANUARY 23

This is my Father's world.
And to my listening ears,
All nature sings and round me rings,
The music of the spheres.

M.D. Babcock

Thank you Father for the indescribable beauty of Your world. Thank You that it is mine to enjoy. Amen.

JULY 24

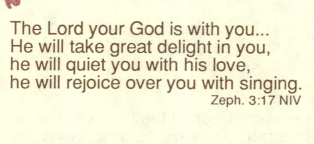

The Lord your God is with you...
He will take great delight in you,
he will quiet you with his love,
he will rejoice over you with singing.

Zeph. 3:17 NIV

*It humbles, yet thrills me to think that You
delight in me, Lord and rejoice over me with
singing! Thank You. Amen.*

JANUARY 24

In the presence of trouble,
some people grow wings;
others buy crutches.

But those who hope in the Lord will renew
their strength. They will soar on wings like
eagles, they will run and not grow weary,
they will walk and not be faint.

Is. 40:31 NIV

JULY 25

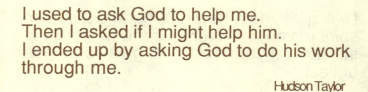

I used to ask God to help me.
Then I asked if I might help him.
I ended up by asking God to do his work
through me.

Hudson Taylor

For God is at work within you... helping
you do what he wants.

Phil. 2:13 TLB

 **JANUARY 25**

I will give you a new heart and put a new spirit in you; I will remove the heart of stone from your flesh and give you a heart of flesh.

Ez. 36:26 NASB

This is my prayer Lord, that my heart will be yielded and made anew. Amen.

JULY 26

...Spend plenty of time with God;
let other things go, but don't neglect Him.

Oswald Chambers

Always give yourselves fully to the work of
the Lord, because you know that your
labor in the Lord is not in vain.

I Cor. 15:58 NIV

JANUARY 26

When I want to speak let me think first:
- Is it true?
- Is it kind?
- Is it necessary?
If not, let it be left unsaid.

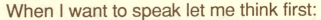

Babcock

When speaking of others this day, I pray for a spirit of kindness. May all my conversation be pleasing in Your sight. Amen.

JULY 27

A wife of noble character, who can find?
She is worth far more than rubies...
Her children arise and call her blessed;
Her husband also, and he praises her.

Prov. 31:10, 28 NIV

JANUARY 27

The first hour of waking is the rudder that guides the whole day.

Henry W. Beecher

Satisfy us in the morning with your unfailing love, that we may sing for joy and be glad all our days.

Ps. 90:14 NIV

JULY 28

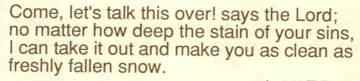

Come, let's talk this over! says the Lord;
no matter how deep the stain of your sins,
I can take it out and make you as clean as
freshly fallen snow.

Is. 1:18 TLB

*Heavenly Father, may the gentle falling of
fresh snow be a reminder to me of what You
can do in my life. Amen.*

JANUARY 28

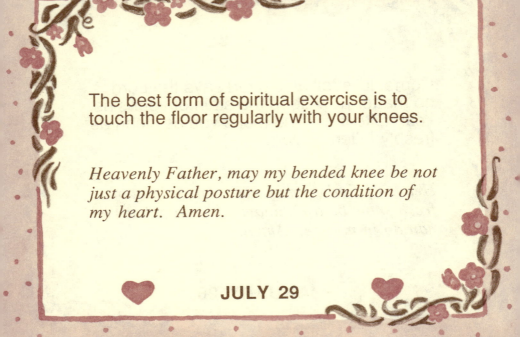

The best form of spiritual exercise is to touch the floor regularly with your knees.

Heavenly Father, may my bended knee be not just a physical posture but the condition of my heart. Amen.

JULY 29

People are like stained glass windows;
they sparkle and shine when the sun is
out, but when the darkness sets in their
true beauty is revealed only if there is a
light within.

Elizabeth Kubler-Ross

*Lord, in quietness and strength may I trust in
You when the times are dark and I feel no
joy. How thankful I am for Your light.
Amen.*

JANUARY 29

The Lord is good.
When trouble comes,
he is the place to go!
And he knows everyone who trusts in him!

Nah. 1:7 TLB

Father, thank You that no matter what is ahead for me, I can be secure because of Your presence. Amen.

JULY 30

Jesus Christ is the same yesterday, today and forever.

Heb. 13:8 TLB

In a changing world, I give You thanks for Your Word that never changes. Amen.

 JANUARY 30

It is impossible for that man to despair who remembers that his Helper is omnipotent.

Jeremy Taylor

Ah, Sovereign Lord, you have made the heavens and the earth by your great power and out-stretched arm. Nothing is too hard for you.

Jer. 32:17 NIV

JULY 31

Those we love are with the Lord,
and the Lord has promised to be with us.
If they are with Him and He is with us,
they cannot be far away.

Peter Marshall

*Thank you Father for this reassurance -
especially when I feel empty and lonely.
Amen.*

 JANUARY 31

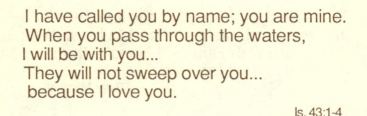

I have called you by name; you are mine.
When you pass through the waters,
I will be with you...
They will not sweep over you...
because I love you.

Is. 43:1-4

Lord, how my heart is filled with thanksgiving as I remember Your promise. Amen.

AUGUST 1

Do what you can, with what you have,
where you are.

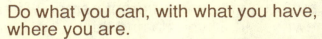

Theodore Roosevelt

I have learned the secret of being content
in any and every situation...
I can do everything through him who gives
me strength.

Phil. 4:12-13 NIV

 FEBRUARY 1

Don't copy the behavior and customs of this world, but be a new and different person with a fresh newness in all you do and think. Then you will learn from your own experience how his ways will really satisfy you.

Rom. 12:2 TLB

May the world not mold me today but may I be so strong as to help mold the world. Amen.

AUGUST 2

In marriage, being the right person is as important as finding the right person.

W.D. Gough

Love always protects, always trusts, always hopes, always perseveres.

I Cor. 13:7 NIV

Lord, give me a loving heart today.   Amen.

FEBRUARY 2

Tears are often the telescope through which men see into heaven.

...weeping may remain for a night,
but rejoicing comes in the morning.

Ps. 30:5 NIV

AUGUST 3

God loves us the way we are,
but he loves us too much to leave us that
way.

Leighton Ford

*Father, if You have any surprise of new truth
or new opportunity for me, make me ready
to meet it with gladness and to use it with
wisdom. Amen.*

 FEBRUARY 3

When I had lost all hope, I turned my thoughts once more to the Lord. My earnest prayer went to you in your Holy Temple.

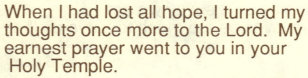

Jonah 2:7 TLB

Lord, my hope is in You. The things that I fear most - I put into Your loving hands, knowing I am safe in Your care. Amen.

AUGUST 4

Love does no wrong to anyone.
That's why it fully satisfies all of God's
requirements. It is the only law you need.

Rom. 13:10 TLB

FEBRUARY 4

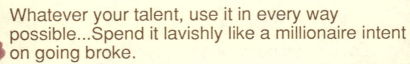

Whatever your talent, use it in every way possible...Spend it lavishly like a millionaire intent on going broke.

Brendan Francis

In everything you do, put God first and he will direct you and crown your efforts with success.

Prov. 3:6 TLB

AUGUST 5

Create in me a new clean heart, O God,
filled with clean thoughts and right desires.

Ps. 51:10 TLB

*Lord, I desire Your Spirit to live within my
heart. Show me my sins, so that I may
change my ways. Amen.*

 **FEBRUARY 5**

Happiness is inward and not outward;
and so it does not depend on what we have,
but on what we are.

Henry Van Dyke

Watch over your heart with all diligence,
For from it flow the springs of life.

Prov. 4:23 NASB

AUGUST 6

You cannot glorify God better
than by a calm and joyous life.
Spurgeon

...for the joy of the Lord is your strength.
Neh. 8:10 NASB

FEBRUARY 6

So don't be anxious about tomorrow.
God will take care of your tomorrow too.
Live one day at a time.

Matt. 6:34 TLB

Father, I thank You for Your loving care. Help me to rest in the hours of today and to entrust the future to You. Amen.

AUGUST 7

But the Lord said...
I don't make decisions the way you do!
Men judge by outward appearance, but I
look at a man's thoughts and intentions.

I Sam. 16:7 TLB

FEBRUARY 7

You may look lightly upon the Scripture and see nothing; meditate often upon it and there you shall see a light like the light of the sun.

Joseph Carly

Your word is a lamp to my feet and a light for my path.

Ps. 119:105 NIV

AUGUST 8

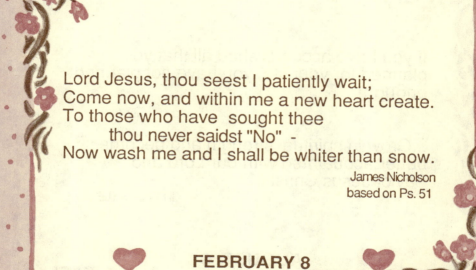

Lord Jesus, thou seest I patiently wait;
Come now, and within me a new heart create.
To those who have sought thee
thou never saidst "No" -
Now wash me and I shall be whiter than snow.

James Nicholson
based on Ps. 51

FEBRUARY 8

If you have accomplished all that you planned for your life, you have not planned enough!

...Grow in spiritual strength and become better acquainted with our Lord and Savior Jesus Christ...

II Pet. 3:18 TLB

 AUGUST 9

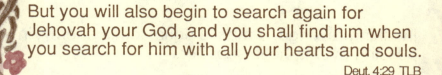

But you will also begin to search again for Jehovah your God, and you shall find him when you search for him with all your hearts and souls.

Deut. 4:29 TLB

Seek the Lord while you can find him. Call upon him now while he is near.

Is. 55:16 TLB

FEBRUARY 9

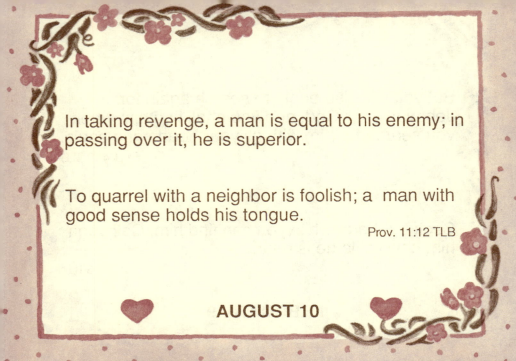

In taking revenge, a man is equal to his enemy; in passing over it, he is superior.

To quarrel with a neighbor is foolish; a man with good sense holds his tongue.

Prov. 11:12 TLB

AUGUST 10

Carefully avoid in yourself those things which disturb you in others.

T. á Kempis

...first take the log out of your own eye, and then you will see clearly to take the speck out of your brother's eye.

Matt. 7:5 RSV

 FEBRUARY 10

Faith is a
        Fantastic
        Adventure
        In
        Trusting
        Him

Corrie ten Boom

AUGUST 11

If you love only those who love you,
what good is that?
...If you are friendly only to your friends,
how are you different from anyone else?...

Matt. 5:46-47 TLB

FEBRUARY 11

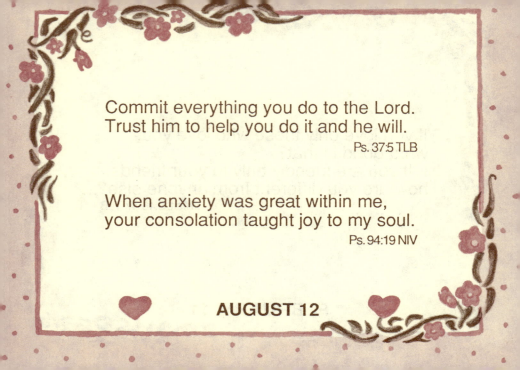

Commit everything you do to the Lord.
Trust him to help you do it and he will.

Ps. 37:5 TLB

When anxiety was great within me,
your consolation taught joy to my soul.

Ps. 94:19 NIV

AUGUST 12

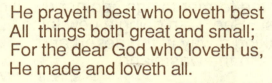

He prayeth best who loveth best
All things both great and small;
For the dear God who loveth us,
He made and loveth all.

Samuel Taylor Coleridge

Now these three remain: faith, hope and love.
But the greatest of these is love.

I Cor. 13:13 NIV

FEBRUARY 12

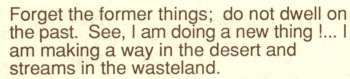

Forget the former things; do not dwell on
the past. See, I am doing a new thing !... I
am making a way in the desert and
streams in the wasteland.

Is. 43:18-19 NIV

*Father, when I trust You, the way is prepared
and my thirst is quenched. Thank You.
Amen.*

AUGUST 13

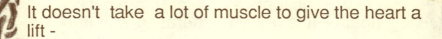

It doesn't take a lot of muscle to give the heart a lift -

...he met him...and encouraged him in his faith in God.

I Sam. 23:16 TLB

 FEBRUARY 13

He who accepts evil without protesting against it is really cooperating with it!

...Find out what pleases the Lord. Have nothing to do with the fruitless deeds of darkness...

Eph. 5:10-11 NIV

AUGUST 14

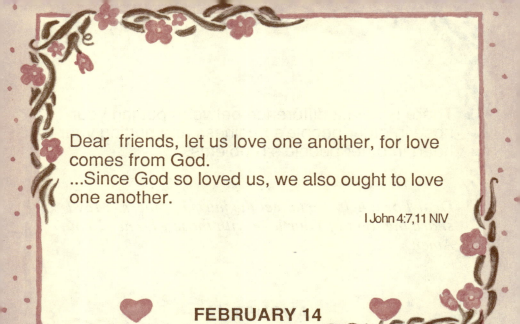

Dear friends, let us love one another, for love comes from God.
...Since God so loved us, we also ought to love one another.

I John 4:7,11 NIV

FEBRUARY 14

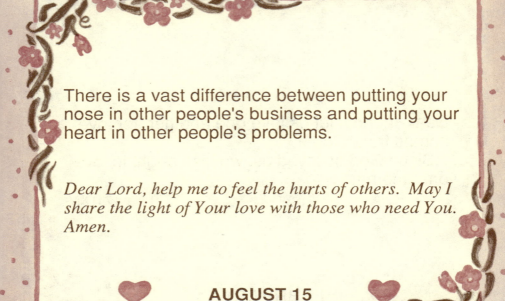

There is a vast difference between putting your nose in other people's business and putting your heart in other people's problems.

Dear Lord, help me to feel the hurts of others. May I share the light of Your love with those who need You. Amen.

AUGUST 15

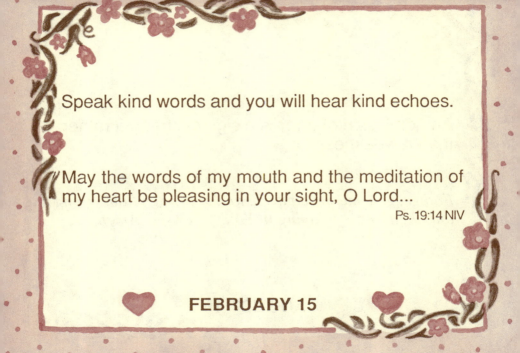

Speak kind words and you will hear kind echoes.

"May the words of my mouth and the meditation of my heart be pleasing in your sight, O Lord...

Ps. 19:14 NIV

FEBRUARY 15

An admission of error is a sign of strength rather than a weakness.

Father, give me the courage to admit when I am wrong and then to go on living in Your freedom. Amen.

AUGUST 16

My prayer for you is that you will overflow more and more with love for others, and at the same time keep on growing in spiritual knowledge and insight.

Phil. 1:9 TLB

Today Lord, make me sensitive and alert to the needs You would have me see. Amen.

 FEBRUARY 16

To believe, and to consent to be loved while unworthy, is the great secret.

W.R. Newell

Lord, I believe. Thank You for Your great love. Amen.

AUGUST 17

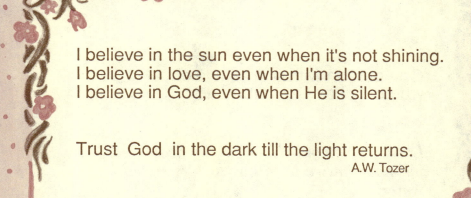

I believe in the sun even when it's not shining.
I believe in love, even when I'm alone.
I believe in God, even when He is silent.

Trust God in the dark till the light returns.

A.W. Tozer

...without faith it is impossible to please God...

Heb. 11:6 NIV

FEBRUARY 17

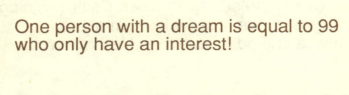

One person with a dream is equal to 99 who only have an interest!

Lord, plant Your dream in my heart and give me Your desire to follow it to completion. Amen.

AUGUST 18

Unless the heart is full, even a rich man is poor.

Love the Lord your God with all your heart and with all your soul and with all your mind and with all your strength.

Mk. 12:30 NIV

 FEBRUARY 18

We are not at our best when we are perched at the summit; we are at our best climbing - even when the way is steep.

Lord, I know that the battles, the uphill climbs must be faced - Help me "Keep to the paths of the righteous". *Amen*.

Prov. 2:20 NIV

 AUGUST 19

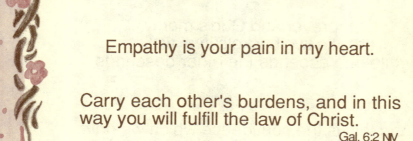

Empathy is your pain in my heart.

Carry each other's burdens, and in this way you will fulfill the law of Christ.

Gal. 6:2 NIV

FEBRUARY 19

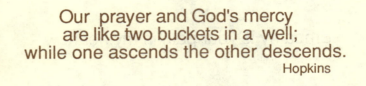

Our prayer and God's mercy
are like two buckets in a well;
while one ascends the other descends.

Hopkins

And this is the confidence which we have
before Him, that, if we ask anything
according to His will, He hears us.

I John 5:14 NASB

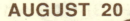

AUGUST 20

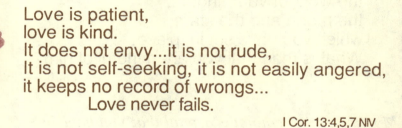

Love is patient,
love is kind.
It does not envy...it is not rude,
It is not self-seeking, it is not easily angered,
it keeps no record of wrongs...
Love never fails.

I Cor. 13:4,5,7 NIV

FEBRUARY 20

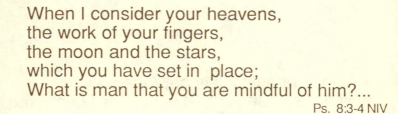

When I consider your heavens,
the work of your fingers,
the moon and the stars,
which you have set in place;
What is man that you are mindful of him?...

Ps. 8:3-4 NIV

My finite mind cannot grasp all that You have in mind for Your creation. This only adds to the joy and expectation of each new day. Amen.

 AUGUST 21

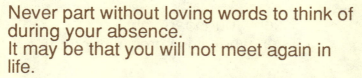

Never part without loving words to think of during your absence.
It may be that you will not meet again in life.

Jean Paul Richter

Father, I often speak without thinking. Help me to guard my words and to speak in love to those I care about. Amen.

FEBRUARY 21

Keep your heart right,
even when it is sorely wounded.

In sorrow Lord, may Your comfort remove all the bitterness and longing. Give me the courage to face this heartache. Thank You. Amen.

AUGUST 22

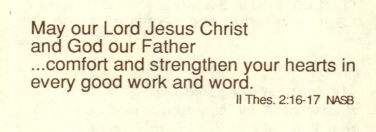

May our Lord Jesus Christ
and God our Father
...comfort and strengthen your hearts in
every good work and word.

II Thes. 2:16-17 NASB

FEBRUARY 22

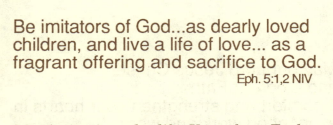

Be imitators of God...as dearly loved children, and live a life of love... as a fragrant offering and sacrifice to God.

Eph. 5:1,2 NIV

My desire is to be like You, dear Father. Please show me how to live the life of love that You have called me to. Amen.

AUGUST 23

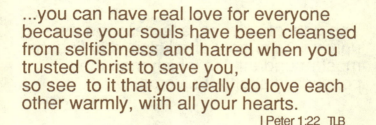

...you can have real love for everyone because your souls have been cleansed from selfishness and hatred when you trusted Christ to save you, so see to it that you really do love each other warmly, with all your hearts.

I Peter 1:22 TLB

Please give me Your love to share with those around me. Amen.

FEBRUARY 23

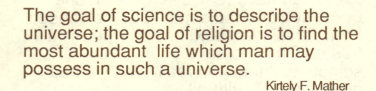

The goal of science is to describe the universe; the goal of religion is to find the most abundant life which man may possess in such a universe.

Kirtely F. Mather

...I came that they might have life and might have it abundantly.

John 10:10 NASB

AUGUST 24

How great is the love the Father
has lavished on us, that we should be
called children of God.

I John 3:1 NIV

And since we are his sons,
everything he has belongs to us,
for that is the way God planned.

Gal. 4:7 TLB

*Words cannot express the gratitude within
my heart when I say - Heavenly Father.
Amen.*

 FEBRUARY 24

Be careful that your victories do not bring with them the seeds of future defeats.

Lord, You know that my heart is not always pure. I confess to You my innermost thoughts. Please forgive me. Amen.

AUGUST 25

People need love,
especially when they don't deserve it.

Thank You Father for Your love - especially
when I don't deserve it - Please help me
follow Your example. Amen.

 FEBRUARY 25

He gives power to the tired and worn out, and strength to the weak.

Is. 40:29 TLB

Come unto me, all you who are weary and burdened, and I willl give you rest.

Matt. 11:28 NIV

 **AUGUST 26**

Just as out of the dark ground comes the blossom, so out of the night, a morning appears.

Father, thank You for the sense of Your presence in the midst of the anxieties of our daily life. Help me to realize Your love for me and to be reminded of it with the dawn of each new day. Amen.

FEBRUARY 26

God has a natural law in force to the effect
that we are conformed to that upon which
we center our interest and love.

Miles Stanford

Thou will keep him in perfect peace,
whose mind is stayed on Thee...

Is. 26:3 KJV

AUGUST 27

Don't act like the people who make
horoscopes and try to read their fate
and future in the stars!
Their ways are futile and foolish.

Jer. 10:2-3 TLB

I have a future all sublime,
Beyond the realms of space and time,
Where my Redeemer I shall see-
And sorrow never more shall be.

Nils Frykman
Tr. A.L. Skoog*

FEBRUARY 27

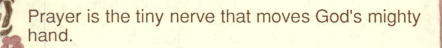

Prayer is the tiny nerve that moves God's mighty hand.

Do not be anxious about anything, but in everything, by prayer... present your requests to God.

Phil. 4:6 NIV

AUGUST 28

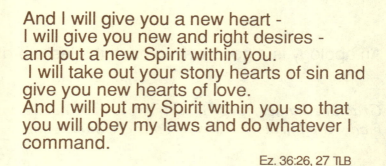

And I will give you a new heart -
I will give you new and right desires -
and put a new Spirit within you.
I will take out your stony hearts of sin and
give you new hearts of love.
And I will put my Spirit within you so that
you will obey my laws and do whatever I
command.

Ez. 36:26, 27 TLB

FEBRUARY 28

An apology is a good way to have the last word!

Gracious Father, forgive me if by word or deed I have made life harder for any of Your creation. Amen.

AUGUST 29

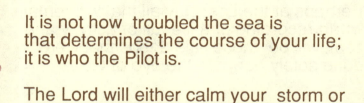

It is not how troubled the sea is
that determines the course of your life;
it is who the Pilot is.

The Lord will either calm your storm or
allow it to rage while He calms you.

...If God is for us - who can be against us?

Rom. 8:31 NIV

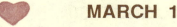

MARCH 1

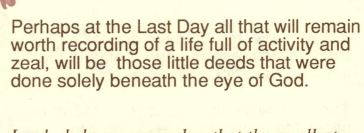

Perhaps at the Last Day all that will remain worth recording of a life full of activity and zeal, will be those little deeds that were done solely beneath the eye of God.

Lord , help me remember that the smallest job done in Your name is very worthwhile. Teach me to rejoice in whatever task is set before me today. Amen.

AUGUST 30

Find your joy in something finished,
And not a thousand things begun.

Douglas Mallock

For if he lays the foundation and is not
able to finish it, everyone who sees it will
ridicule him.

Luke 14:29 NIV

MARCH 2

He has the film of my whole life in view,
and not just the snapshot of my present
situation.

W. Trobisch

*O Lord, I get lost in the "dailyness" of life.
Please help me see Your perspective. Amen.*

AUGUST 31

Soft-hearted instead of hard-headed...
that's what love is about.

And be kind to one another, tender-
hearted, forgiving each other, just as God
in Christ also has forgiven you.

Eph. 4:32 NASB

MARCH 3

He who runs from God in the morning
will scarcely find him the rest of the day.

Bunyan

And in the early morning,
   while it was still dark,
He rose and went out and departed to a
lonely place, and was praying there.

Mark 1:35 NASB

 SEPTEMBER 1

In this new life one's nationality or race or education or social position is unimportant,
...whether a person has Christ is what matters, and he is equally available to all.

Col. 3:11 TLB

Father, the world is so full of need. Break down barriers that would keep us from showing Your love to all mankind. Amen.

MARCH 4

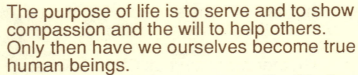

The purpose of life is to serve and to show compassion and the will to help others. Only then have we ourselves become true human beings.

Albert Schweitzer

Lord, make me conscious of the needs of those who hurt. Help me not to count the cost of serving You but to be willing to reach out to those You direct me to today. Amen.

SEPTEMBER 2

Our voluntary thoughts not only reveal what we are, they predict what we will become.

A.W. Tozer

Grant us, O Lord, that we may never forget Whose we are and Whom we serve. Amen.

 MARCH 5

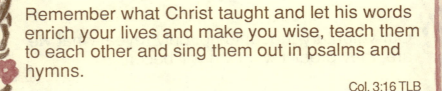

Remember what Christ taught and let his words enrich your lives and make you wise, teach them to each other and sing them out in psalms and hymns.

Col. 3:16 TLB

Lord, let me fill my thoughts with Your words and live so close to You that Your wisdom will become a permanent part of my life. Amen.

 SEPTEMBER 3

If all our misfortunes were laid in one common heap,
most people would be contented to take their own and depart.

Father, I ask that you remove these feelings of self pity. Heal me of their scars. Please put self-respect and a sense of my many blessings in their place. Amen.

MARCH 6

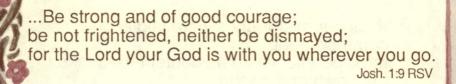

...Be strong and of good courage;
be not frightened, neither be dismayed;
for the Lord your God is with you wherever you go.

Josh. 1:9 RSV

In my mind I limit You so often Lord. I lose sight of the fact that You are always with me and have given me the gift of Your love. Thank You Lord. Amen.

SEPTEMBER 4

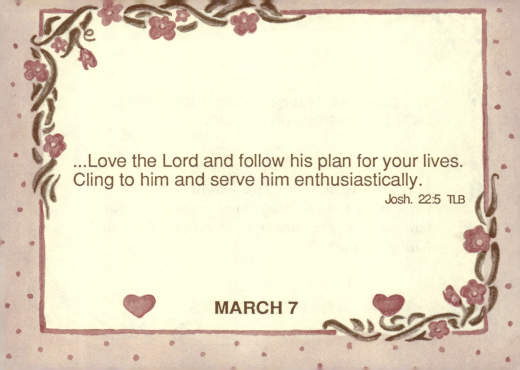

...Love the Lord and follow his plan for your lives. Cling to him and serve him enthusiastically.

Josh. 22:5 TLB

MARCH 7

We have, all of us, sufficient fortitude to bear the misfortunes of others.

La Rochefoucould

Lord, show me who You would have me walk with today. Help me remember Your teaching to "encourage each other". In Jesus' Name. Amen.

SEPTEMBER 5

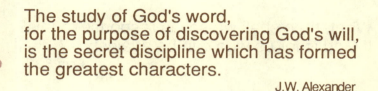

The study of God's word,
for the purpose of discovering God's will,
is the secret discipline which has formed
the greatest characters.

J.W. Alexander

Thy word have I hid in my heart that I may
not sin against thee.

Ps. 119:11 KJV

MARCH 8

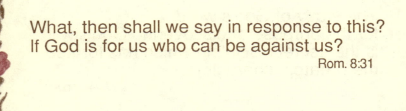

What, then shall we say in response to this?
If God is for us who can be against us?

Rom. 8:31

*Indeed Lord! How comforting it is to be
reminded that we will succeed when we are on
Your side. Amen.*

SEPTEMBER 6

There is no pillow so soft as a clear conscience.
French Proverb

Lord, if I have hurt or offended someone today, give me the courage to make it right before I go to sleep tonight. Amen.

MARCH 9

Christianity is a battle,
not a dream.

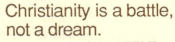

Wendell Phillips

Pursue righteousness, godliness, faith, love,
endurance and gentleness. Fight the good fight
of faith. Take hold of eternal life.

I Tim 6:12 NIV

 SEPTEMBER 7

...We know that all that happens to us is working for our good if we love God and are fitting into his plans.

Rom 8:28 TLB

Lord, I can face the future with confidence, knowing that all the events of all my tomorrows are in Your loving hands. For this hope, I thank You. Amen.

MARCH 10

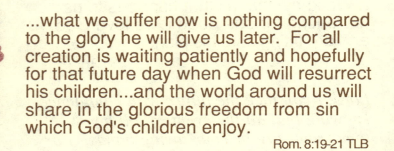

...what we suffer now is nothing compared to the glory he will give us later. For all creation is waiting patiently and hopefully for that future day when God will resurrect his children...and the world around us will share in the glorious freedom from sin which God's children enjoy.

Rom. 8:19-21 TLB

SEPTEMBER 8

Be cheerful! Of all the things you wear, your expression is the most important.

A happy heart makes the face cheerful...
Prov. 15:13 NIV

MARCH 11

There is only one limit to what prayer can do;
that is what God can do.

R.A. Torrey

Is anything too hard for the Lord?...
Gen. 18:14 RSV

SEPTEMBER 9

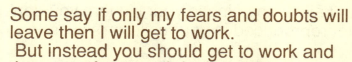

Some say if only my fears and doubts will leave then I will get to work.
 But instead you should get to work and then your fears and doubts will leave.

D.L. Moody

...He who began a good work in you will carry it on to completion...

Phil. 1:6 NIV

MARCH 12

Don't allow anything in your life that you don't want reproduced in your children's lives.

Father, help me remember this day that younger eyes are watching my behavior. Please help me be the example that will be pleasing to You and that will draw others to You. Amen.

SEPTEMBER 10

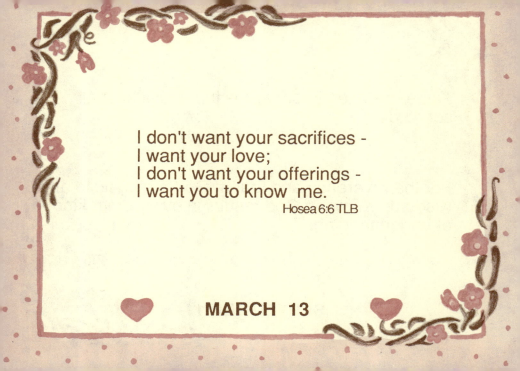

I don't want your sacrifices -
I want your love;
I don't want your offerings -
I want you to know me.

Hosea 6:6 TLB

MARCH 13

To be enslaved to oneself is the heaviest of all servitudes.

Seneca

For the reverence and fear of God are basic to all wisdom. Knowing God results in every other kind of understanding.

Prov. 9:10 TLB

SEPTEMBER 11

Our little time of suffering is not worthy of our first night's welcome home to Heaven.

Samuel Rutherford

Lord Jesus, thank You for the hope and assurance of a heavenly home. Let this hope be reflected in my life today. Amen.

MARCH 14

Leisure is a beautiful garment,
but it will not do for constant wear.

For six days, work is to be done, but the seventh
day shall be your holy day, a Sabbath of rest to
the Lord.

Ex. 35:2 NIV

SEPTEMBER 12

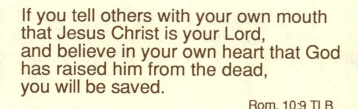

If you tell others with your own mouth
that Jesus Christ is your Lord,
and believe in your own heart that God
has raised him from the dead,
you will be saved.

Rom. 10:9 TLB

Faith is a gift - but you **can** ask for it.
Fulton Oursler

MARCH 15

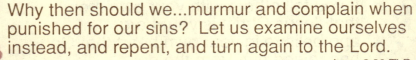

Why then should we...murmur and complain when punished for our sins? Let us examine ourselves instead, and repent, and turn again to the Lord.

Lam. 3:39 TLB

Help me remember that there are always consequences to my actions. Give me the strength to choose Your way. Amen.

SEPTEMBER 13

Years may wrinkle the skin,
but to give up interest wrinkles the soul.
Douglas MacArthur

Lord, keep me growing and changing to
become the person You desire me to be.
Amen.

MARCH 16

A lasting work requires extensive preparation.

Douglas Rumford

Lord, help me see Your hand of preparation in my life.
Create in me a lasting work. Amen.

SEPTEMBER 14

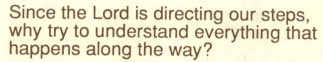

Since the Lord is directing our steps,
why try to understand everything that
happens along the way?

Prov. 20:24 TLB

Trust in the Lord with all your heart and
lean not on your own understanding.

Prov. 3:5 NIV

 **MARCH 17**

The great point is to never give up until the answer comes...

The great fault of the children of God is, they do not continue in prayer...they do not persevere.

If they desire anything for God's glory, they should pray until they get it.

George Mueller

 SEPTEMBER 15

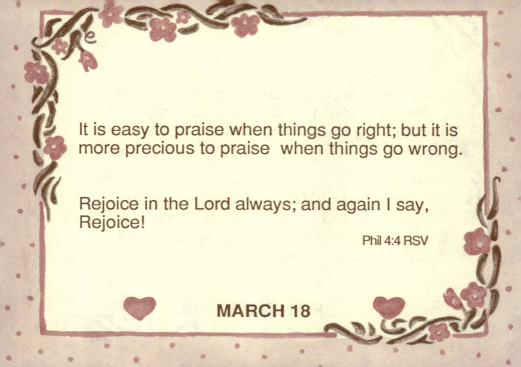

It is easy to praise when things go right; but it is more precious to praise when things go wrong.

Rejoice in the Lord always; and again I say, Rejoice!

Phil 4:4 RSV

MARCH 18

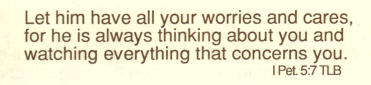

Let him have all your worries and cares, for he is always thinking about you and watching everything that concerns you.

I Pet. 5:7 TLB

This is incredible, Lord, and so comforting! Teach me to keep my eyes on You and to allow You to give me peace of heart and mind today. Amen.

  SEPTEMBER 16

It is possible to give without loving,
but it is impossible to love without giving.

R. Braunstein

He who did not hesitate to spare his own
Son but gave him up for us all - can we not
trust such a God to give us, with Him,
everything else that we can need?

Rom. 8:32 Phillips

MARCH 19

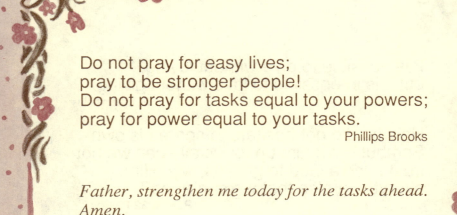

Do not pray for easy lives;
pray to be stronger people!
Do not pray for tasks equal to your powers;
pray for power equal to your tasks.

Phillips Brooks

Father, strengthen me today for the tasks ahead.
Amen.

SEPTEMBER 17

Don't worry about opposition. Remember, a kite rises against the wind, not with the wind.

Hamilton Wright Mabie

...let us run with endurance the race that is set before us, fixing our eyes on Jesus...

Heb. 12:1-2 NASB

MARCH 20

You are not tempted because you are evil;
you are tempted because you are human.

So give yourselves humbly to God.
Resist the devil and he will flee from you.

James 4:7 TLB

SEPTEMBER 18

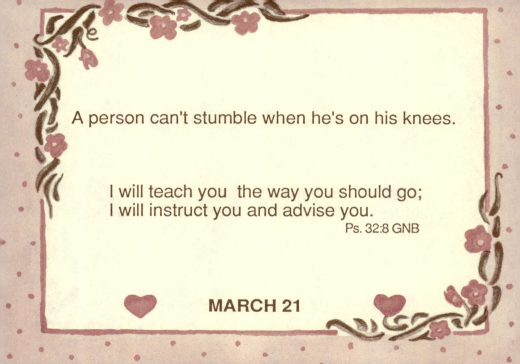

A person can't stumble when he's on his knees.

I will teach you the way you should go;
I will instruct you and advise you.

Ps. 32:8 GNB

MARCH 21

Getting me into hot water is often God's way of keeping me clean.

Create in me a new, clean heart, O God, filled with clean thoughts and right desires.

Ps. 51:10 TLB

SEPTEMBER 19

God uses men who are weak and feeble enough to lean on Him.

Hudson Taylor

...My grace is sufficient for you, for my power is made perfect in weakness. Therefore, I will boast...about my weaknesses, so that Christ's power may rest on me.

II Cor. 12:9 NIV

MARCH 22

A man's character is like a fence -
it cannot be strengthened by whitewash.

Fear not, for I am with you,
 be not dismayed, for I am your God;
I will strengthen you, I will help you,
I will uphold you with my victorious right hand.

Is. 41:10 RSV

 SEPTEMBER 20

Poverty is life without Jesus, but close friendship with Him is incalculable wealth.

T. á Kempis

Now change your mind and attitude to God and turn to him...

Acts 3:19 TLB

MARCH 23

Normal day -
- let me be aware of the treasure you are!

SEPTEMBER 21

We are never more discontented with others than when we are discontented with ourselves.

Lord, when I am critical of others, cause me to stop and examine myself. Amen.

 MARCH 24

He is no fool who gives what he cannot keep to gain what he cannot lose.

Jim Elliot

Father, give me the courage to give myself to You to gain eternal life. Amen.

 SEPTEMBER 22

A little faith will bring your soul to heaven, but great faith will bring heaven to your soul.

Spurgeon

Now faith is the assurance of things hoped for, the conviction of things not seen.

Heb. 11:1 NASB

MARCH 25

Happiness is a perfume you can't pour on others without getting a few drops on yourself.

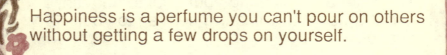

...all who fear God and trust in him are blessed beyond expression. Yes, happy is the man who delights in doing his commands.

Ps. 112:1 TLB

 SEPTEMBER 23

We despised him and rejected him;
he endured suffering and pain...
he endured the suffering that should have
been ours,
the pain we should have borne.

Is. 53:3 GNB

*Lord, it was for me that You were despised
and rejected. Search my heart and show me
if today I am part of that rejection. Amen.*

MARCH 26

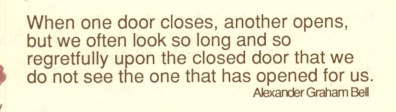

When one door closes, another opens, but we often look so long and so regretfully upon the closed door that we do not see the one that has opened for us.

Alexander Graham Bell

Show me Your path Lord. Help me be so attuned to Your will that I will experience all that You have for me. Amen.

SEPTEMBER 24

And they crucified Him...
Matt. 28:35 KJV

I thank You, Lord, for taking the worst that could have happened at the hands of sinful men and turning it into the world's greatest victory, available to all who accept it. Amen.

MARCH 27

The world is poor because her treasure is buried in the sky and all her treasure maps are of the earth.

Calvin Miller

Dear Lord, help me keep my eyes on You and off of the things of this earth. Amen.

 SEPTEMBER 25

How precious it is, Lord, to realize that you are thinking about me constantly...

Ps. 139:17 TLB

O Lord, please don't ever let me think that I can stand by myself and not need You. Amen.

MARCH 28

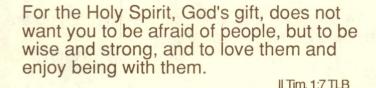

For the Holy Spirit, God's gift, does not want you to be afraid of people, but to be wise and strong, and to love them and enjoy being with them.

II Tim. 1:7 TLB

Lord, whatever I fear most, I give to You; trusting that You will give me Your peace and courage. Amen.

 SEPTEMBER 26

Grace to you and peace from God our
Father and the Lord Jesus Christ.

I I Cor. 1:2 NASB

What a wonderful God we have...
who so wonderfully strengthens us in our
hardships and trials. And why does he do
this?
So that when others are troubled, needing
our sympathy and encouragement, we
can pass on to them this same help and
comfort God has given us.

II Cor. 1:3-4 TLB

MARCH 29

In prayer it is better to have a heart without words than words without heart.

John Bunyan

Father, keep my heart soft this day and fill it with Your thoughts. Amen.

 SEPTEMBER 27

Words which do not give the light of Christ
increase the darkness...

Mother Theresa

His life is the light that shines through darkness-

John 1:5 TLB

MARCH 30

The way to gain a good reputation is to endeavor to be what you desire to appear.

Let us not become weary in doing good, for at the proper time we will reap a harvest if we do not give up.

Gal. 6:9 NIV

 SEPTEMBER 28

And he said,
 "My presence will go with you, and I will
give you rest."

Ex. 33:14 RSV

We are so busy Lord - how easy it is to become overwhelmed - Thank You for Your promise of rest.   Amen.

MARCH 31

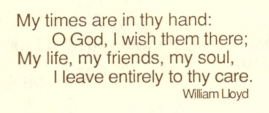

My times are in thy hand:
　　O God, I wish them there;
My life, my friends, my soul,
　　I leave entirely to thy care.

William Lloyd

I am leaving you with a gift - peace of mind and heart!... So, don't be troubled or afraid.

John 14:27 TLB

SEPTEMBER 29

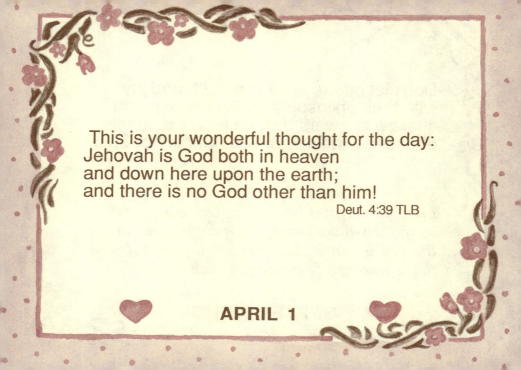

This is your wonderful thought for the day:
Jehovah is God both in heaven
and down here upon the earth;
and there is no God other than him!

Deut. 4:39 TLB

APRIL 1

Don't let others spoil your faith and joy with their philosophies, their wrong and shallow answers built on men's thoughts and ideas, instead of what Christ has said.

Col. 2:8 TLB

Lord, how can it be that in our search, men so quickly pass You by? Open my eyes to see the Truth and make me ready to share it with those who are searching. Amen.

 SEPTEMBER 30

The essence of genius is to know what to overlook.

William James

Forgetting what is behind and straining toward what is ahead, I press on toward the goal to win the prize for which God has called me heavenward in Christ Jesus.

Phil. 3:13-14 NIV

APRIL 2

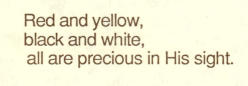

Red and yellow,
black and white,
 all are precious in His sight.

God made you as you are in order to use you as
He planned.

S.C. McAulay

OCTOBER 1

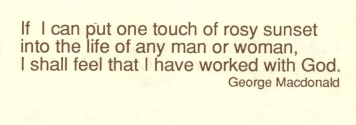

If I can put one touch of rosy sunset
into the life of any man or woman,
I shall feel that I have worked with God.

George Macdonald

*Lord, make me sensitive to the needs and
feelings of others. Amen.*

APRIL 3

Great works are performed not by strength, but by perserverance.

Samuel Johnson

...let us run with perservance the race marked out for us.

Heb. 12:1 NIV

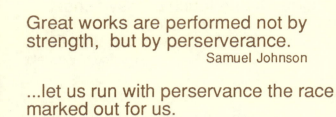

OCTOBER 2

...but the angel said, "Don't be so surprised. Aren't you looking for Jesus... He isn't here! He has come back to life!"

Mark 16:6 TLB

Lives again our glorious King...
Where, O death, is thy sting?...
Dying once He all doth save,...
Where thy victory, O grave?...

Charles Wesley

APRIL 4

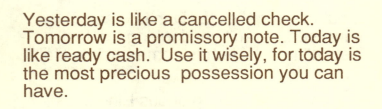

Yesterday is like a cancelled check. Tomorrow is a promissory note. Today is like ready cash. Use it wisely, for today is the most precious possession you can have.

Lord, give me a sense of Your direction. May I use today wisely and realize the value of each new day You give me. Amen.

OCTOBER 3

...Lo, I am with you always,
even unto the end of the world.
Matt. 28:20 KJV

*I yearn to keep the precious blessing of
Easter in my heart throughout the year. I ask
that You fill my heart with the knowledge
and surety that You live. Amen.*

APRIL 5

Never report what may hurt another, unless it be a greater hurt to some other to conceal it.

William Penn

Do not let any unwholesome talk come out of your mouths, only what is helpful for building others up...

Eph. 4:29 NIV

OCTOBER 4

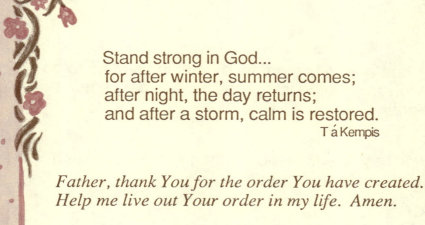

Stand strong in God...
for after winter, summer comes;
after night, the day returns;
and after a storm, calm is restored.

T á Kempis

Father, thank You for the order You have created.
Help me live out Your order in my life. Amen.

APRIL 6

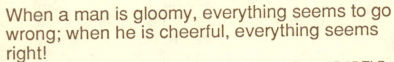

When a man is gloomy, everything seems to go wrong; when he is cheerful, everything seems right!

Prov. 15:15 TLB

Delight yourself in the Lord and he will give you the desires of your heart.

Ps. 37:4 NIV

 OCTOBER 5

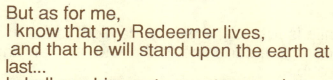

But as for me,
I know that my Redeemer lives,
 and that he will stand upon the earth at
last...
I shall see him, not as a stranger, but as a
friend.
What a glorious hope!
Amen!

Job 19:25-27 TLB

APRIL 7

A smile is rest to the weary, daylight to the discouraged, sunshine to the sad, and an antidote for trouble.

Today, please remind me to spend my smiles lavishly. Amen.

OCTOBER 6

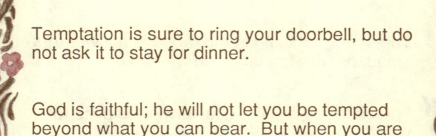

Temptation is sure to ring your doorbell, but do not ask it to stay for dinner.

God is faithful; he will not let you be tempted beyond what you can bear. But when you are tempted, he will also provide a way out...

I Cor. 10:13 NIV

APRIL 8

The important thing in this world is not where we stand, but in what direction we move.

Goethe

I press on toward the goal to win the prize for which God has called me...

Phil 3:14 NIV

OCTOBER 7

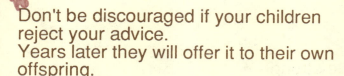

Don't be discouraged if your children
reject your advice.
Years later they will offer it to their own
offspring.

And you must think constantly about these
commandments I am giving you today.
You must teach them to your children
and talk about them when you are at
home or out on a walk; at bedtime and the
first thing in the morning.

Deut. 6:6-7 TLB

APRIL 9

Be strong!
Be courageous!
Do not be afraid...
For the Lord your God will be with you.
He will neither fail you nor forsake you.

Deut. 31:6 TLB

OCTOBER 8

You need not cry very loud;
He is nearer to us than we think.

Brother Lawrence

The good man does not escape all
troubles - he has them too.
But the Lord helps him in each and every
one.

Ps. 34:19 TLB

APRIL 10

May the outward and inward man be one.

Socrates

If anyone considers himself religious and
yet does not keep a tight rein on his
tongue, he deceives himself...

James 1:26 NIV

OCTOBER 9

Friendship is a cozy shelter
from life's rainy days.

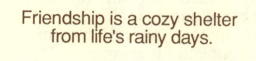

Father, thank you for putting into my life the
dear friends that add so much sunshine.
Amen.

 **APRIL 11**

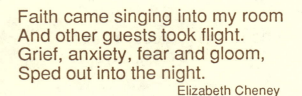

Faith came singing into my room
And other guests took flight.
Grief, anxiety, fear and gloom,
Sped out into the night.

Elizabeth Cheney

Lord, this day may I stay close to You and rest in the
calmness of Your presence. Amen.

OCTOBER 10

Whether you turn to the right or to the left, your ears will hear a voice behind you, saying,

"This is the way - walk in it."

Is. 30:21 NIV

Thank You Father that I can count on You when the job seems too hard, the road seems too long, the load is too heavy, or when I am afraid to go on alone. Amen.

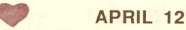

APRIL 12

God has given each of you some special abilities; be sure to use them to help each other, passing on to others God's many kinds of blessings.

I Peter 4:10 TLB

Every talent that I have, You have given me Lord. May I have the wisdom to use these abilities to Your glory. Amen.

OCTOBER 11

There is wonder in the air when I am free to live for today.

Lord, I commit myself to Your care and keeping this day. Amen.

APRIL 13

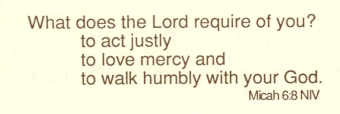

What does the Lord require of you?
    to act justly
    to love mercy and
    to walk humbly with your God.

Micah 6:8 NIV

Lord, keep me walking so close to You that I will reflect Your character in all that I do. Amen.

OCTOBER 12

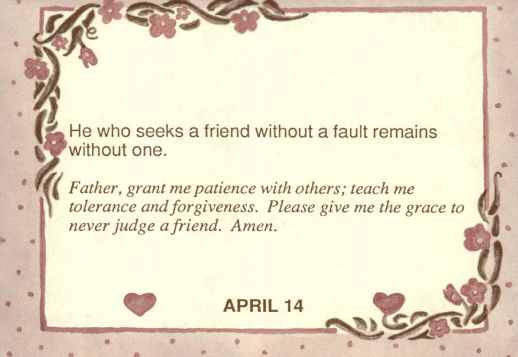

He who seeks a friend without a fault remains without one.

Father, grant me patience with others; teach me tolerance and forgiveness. Please give me the grace to never judge a friend. Amen.

APRIL 14

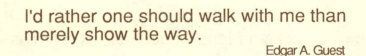

I'd rather one should walk with me than merely show the way.

Edgar A. Guest

If we walk in the light, as he is in the light, we have fellowship with one another.

I John 1:7 NIV

OCTOBER 13

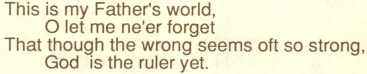

This is my Father's world,
    O let me ne'er forget
That though the wrong seems oft so strong,
    God is the ruler yet.

M. D. Babcock

But the Lord is faithful,
he will strengthen and protect you from
the evil one.

II Thes. 3:3 NIV

APRIL 15

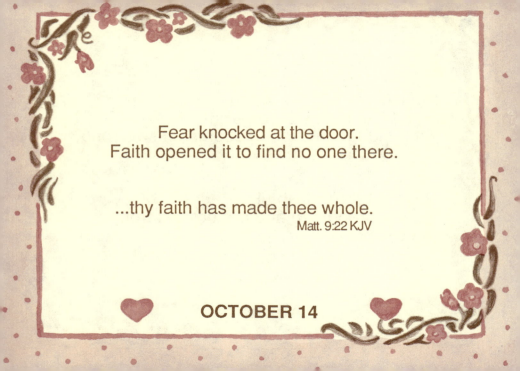

Fear knocked at the door.
Faith opened it to find no one there.

...thy faith has made thee whole.
Matt. 9:22 KJV

OCTOBER 14

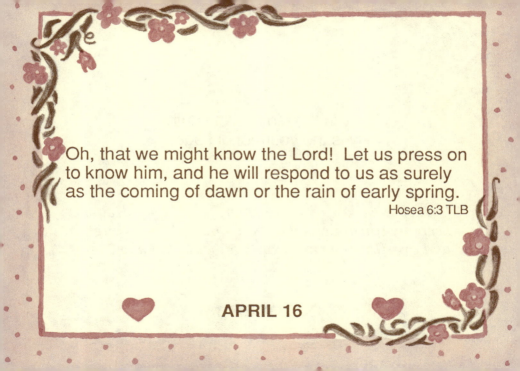

Oh, that we might know the Lord! Let us press on to know him, and he will respond to us as surely as the coming of dawn or the rain of early spring.

Hosea 6:3 TLB

APRIL 16

Forty is the old age of youth;
Fifty is the youth of old age.

Victor Hugo

Lord, please keep me from fearing old age. Help me keep my spirit yielded to You, open to new thoughts and overflowing with words of beauty. Amen.

 OCTOBER 15

Nothing is worth more than this day.
Goethe

Make me aware, Lord, that today never returns. Give me a sense of stewardship that will make me want to use it to count for You. Amen.

This is the day the Lord has made.
Let us rejoice and be glad in it.
Ps. 118:24 NIV

APRIL 17

The steadfast love of the Lord never ceases, his mercies never come to an end; they are new every morning. Great is thy faithfulness!!

Lam. 3:22-23 RSV

Jesus, thank You for Your unchanging love. Even if everyone else changes, I know that You will always be the same. Amen.

OCTOBER 16

Remember not only to say the right thing in the right place, but far more difficult still, to leave unsaid the wrong thing at the tempting moment.

Benjamin Franklin

Please guard my mouth this day, O Lord. Amen.

APRIL 18

It isn't the load that weighs us down - it's the way we carry it.

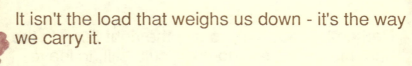

Father, thank You that You carry my burdens for me if I will give them to You. Give me the courage today to lay them at Your feet -and help me not to pick them up again tomorrow! Amen.

OCTOBER 17

A man wrapped up in himself makes a very small package.

If you want favor with both God and man, and a reputation for good judgment and common sense, then trust the Lord completely. Don't ever trust yourself.

Prov. 3:4 TLB

APRIL 19

...to the extent that you did it to one of these brothers of Mine, even the least of them, you did it to Me.

Matt. 25:40 NASB

Father - how hard it is in our busy lives to take time for each other - to show kindness. Help me find time and to know in that moment that I am reaching out to You. Amen.

OCTOBER 18

This Good News tells us that God makes us ready for heaven...when we put our faith and trust in Christ to save us. This is accommplished from start to finish by faith.

Rom. 1:17 TLB

Thank You, Jesus, for this hope of seeing You face to face and the faith You have given me to believe. Amen..

APRIL 20

God's way may be harder for you,
but it will be easier on you.

H. Hanson

I have told you all this so that you will have
peace of heart and mind. Here on earth
you will have many trials and sorrows; but
cheer up, for I have overcome the world.

John 16:33 TLB

OCTOBER 19

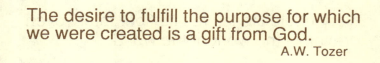

The desire to fulfill the purpose for which we were created is a gift from God.

A.W. Tozer

Dear Father, help me to be open to Your purpose for my life and please give me the desire to fulfill that purpose- starting today. Amen.

APRIL 21

Every noble life leaves its fiber interwoven forever in the work of the world.

Ruskin

Father, help me to share Your joy with someone around me today. Amen.

OCTOBER 20

The highest wisdom is kindness.

Talmud

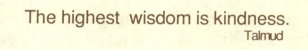

But the wisdom that comes from heaven is
first of all pure and full of quiet
gentleness...it is peace-loving and
courteous.

James 3:17 NIV

APRIL 22

...for being saved is a gift; if a person could earn it by being good, then it wouldn't be free - but it is!... God declares sinners to be good in his sight if they have faith in Christ.

Rom. 4:4,5 TLB

Jesus, thank You for Your glorious gift, Your sacrifice on the cross. You have made me good in God's sight. Amen.

OCTOBER 21

It is ever true that he who does nothing for others does nothing for himself.

Goethe

Lord, make me aware of someone today who could use my encouragement or helping hand. Help me to take the time to be Your messenger. Amen.

APRIL 23

The secret of happy living is not to do what you like but to like what you do.

Lord, be with me in my daily work and help me to take pleasure in each task. Amen.

OCTOBER 22

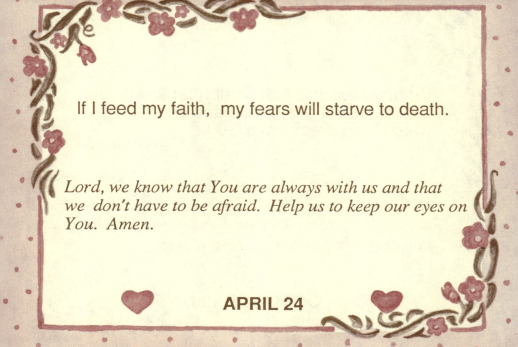

If I feed my faith, my fears will starve to death.

Lord, we know that You are always with us and that we don't have to be afraid. Help us to keep our eyes on You. Amen.

APRIL 24

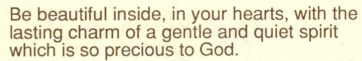

Be beautiful inside, in your hearts, with the lasting charm of a gentle and quiet spirit which is so precious to God.

I Pet. 3:4 TLB

Heavenly Father, help me to grow lovely as I grow older, remembering that growing older makes me but closer to You. Amen.

OCTOBER 23

When morning gilds the skies,
My heart awakening cries,
May Jesus Christ be praised.

Tr. Edward Caswall

Heavenly Father, this is my song as I face this new day.
Amen.

APRIL 25

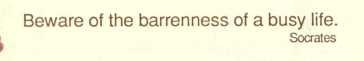

Beware of the barrenness of a busy life.

Socrates

Heavenly Father, help me be diligent in maintaining a meaningful inner life, remembering that time spent with You gives meaning and fruitfulness to my life. Amen.

 OCTOBER 24

What most of all hinders the spiritually minded is that they pay so little heed to small sins..

von Magdeburg

Lord, enlighten me with Your goodness, so that in the secrets of my heart, no dark desires may abide. Amen.

APRIL 26

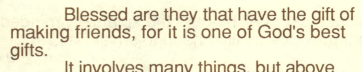

Blessed are they that have the gift of making friends, for it is one of God's best gifts.

It involves many things, but above all, the power of going out of one's self, and appreciating whatever is noble and loving in another.

Thomas Hughes

OCTOBER 25

In acceptance there is peace.

*Lord, I don't pray for tranquility, or that my problems
may cease; I pray that Your Spirit and love would give
me the strength to abide in You during adversity.
Amen.*

APRIL 27

Full-grown oaks are not produced in three years; neither are servants of God.

Douglas Rumford

Lord, please start today shaping me into one of Your servants. Amen.

 OCTOBER 26

What happiness for those whose guilt has been forgiven! What joys when sins are covered over! What relief for those who have confessed their sins and God has cleared their record.

Ps. 32:1,2. TLB

APRIL 28

It is futile to wish for a long life, and then to give so little care to living well.

T. a Kempis

Teach us to number our days that we may gain a heart of wisdom. *Amen.*

Ps. 90:12 NIV

 OCTOBER 27

For the eyes of the Lord are intently watching all who live good lives, and he gives attention when they cry to him.

Ps. 34:15 TLB

How comforting it is, Father, to know that You watch over me. May I live confidently in a sense of Your Presence. Amen.

APRIL 29

Charm is deceptive, and beauty is fleeting; but a woman who fears the Lord is to be praised. Give her the reward she has earned.

Prov. 31: 30,31 NIV

Father, thank You for the example of a godly woman that You have put in my life. Give me the strength to put into practice what I have learned at her knee. Amen.

OCTOBER 28

God won't send us where he is unable to sustain us!

What a glorious Lord! He who daily bears our burdens also gives us our salvation.

Ps. 68:19 TLB

APRIL 30

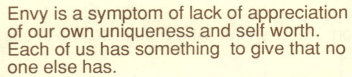

Envy is a symptom of lack of appreciation
of our own uniqueness and self worth.
Each of us has something to give that no
one else has.

Elizabeth O'Connor

Almighty God, stir up the gift within me for
the sake of Thy Kingdom. Amen.

OCTOBER 29

Anxious hearts are very heavy but a word of encouragement does wonders!

Prov. 12:23 TLB

Father, what power is available in a few simple words of encouragement. Remind me to be an encourager in the lives of others. Amen.

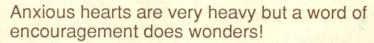

MAY 1

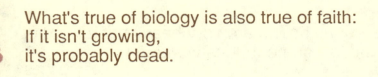

What's true of biology is also true of faith:
If it isn't growing,
it's probably dead.

Let your roots grow down into him and draw
up nourishment from him. See that you go
on growing in the Lord.

Col. 2:7 TLB

OCTOBER 30

No one applauds the fiddle after the concert - they only applaud the fiddler.

Acknowledge the fiddler in your life!

Dear Lord, help me to recognize Your working in my life and to give You thanks for whatever comes my way. Amen.

MAY 2

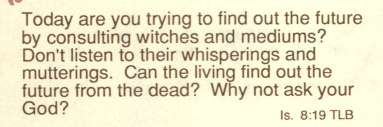

Today are you trying to find out the future by consulting witches and mediums? Don't listen to their whisperings and mutterings. Can the living find out the future from the dead? Why not ask your God?

Is. 8:19 TLB

Dear Lord, our world has so many false ideas. Sometimes I forget to come to You. I ask You this day to protect me from being misled and misguided. Amen.

OCTOBER 31

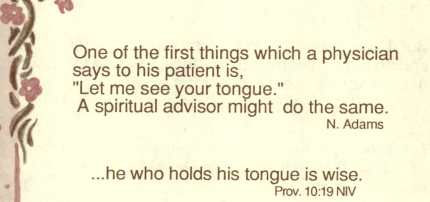

One of the first things which a physician
says to his patient is,
"Let me see your tongue."
A spiritual advisor might do the same.

N. Adams

...he who holds his tongue is wise.

Prov. 10:19 NIV

MAY 3

But if you are unwilling to obey the Lord, then decide today whom you will obey... But as for me and my family, we will serve the Lord.

Josh. 24:15 TLB

Let Your Light so shine in my home today, that those who dwell therein will receive something of Your radiance. Amen.

NOVEMBER 1

Don't be impatient. Wait for the Lord,
and he will come and save you!
Be brave, stouthearted and courageous.
Yes, wait and he will help you.

Ps. 27:14 TLB

*Lord, help me to learn to wait in confidence
for You. I give You my impatience this day.
May I rest in Your love. Amen.*

MAY 4

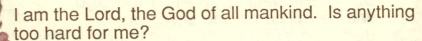

I am the Lord, the God of all mankind. Is anything too hard for me?

Jer. 32:27 NIV

Father, please forgive me when I lose sight of who You are. Amen.

NOVEMBER 2

If I had a single flower for everytime I think about you, I could walk forever in my garden.

Claudia Grandi

Almighty God, help me to be aware that every friend is a gift from You and to be cherished. Amen.

MAY 5

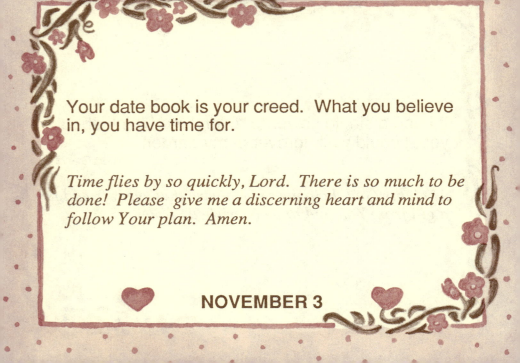

Your date book is your creed. What you believe in, you have time for.

Time flies by so quickly, Lord. There is so much to be done! Please give me a discerning heart and mind to follow Your plan. Amen.

NOVEMBER 3

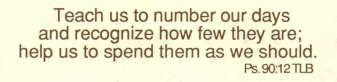

Teach us to number our days
and recognize how few they are;
help us to spend them as we should.
Ps. 90:12 TLB

*O Lord, You know how busy I get every day;
often I lose sight of what is really important.
Help me spend the day according to Your
plan. Amen.*

MAY 6

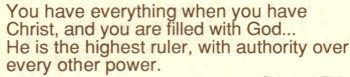

You have everything when you have Christ, and you are filled with God... He is the highest ruler, with authority over every other power.

Col . 2:10 TLB

It is good for me Lord, to think about the wonderful things You have done. May my life overflow with gratitude today. Amen.

NOVEMBER 4

Treat arguments like weeds...
nip them in the bud.

In everything you do, stay away from
complaining and arguing, so that no one
can speak a word of blame against you...

Phil. 2:14 TLB

MAY 7

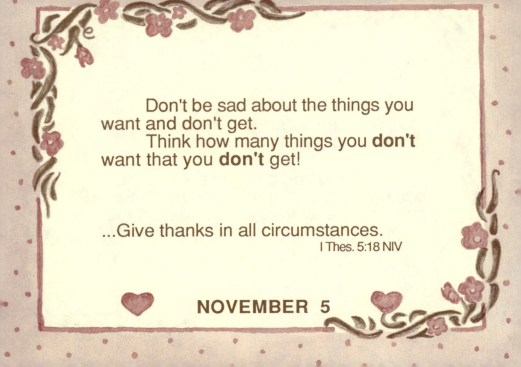

Don't be sad about the things you want and don't get.
Think how many things you **don't** want that you **don't** get!

...Give thanks in all circumstances.

I Thes. 5:18 NIV

NOVEMBER 5

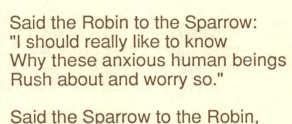

Said the Robin to the Sparrow:
"I should really like to know
Why these anxious human beings
Rush about and worry so."

Said the Sparrow to the Robin,
"Friend, I think that it must be,
That they have no heavenly Father,
Such as cares for you and me."

Elizabeth Cheney

MAY 8

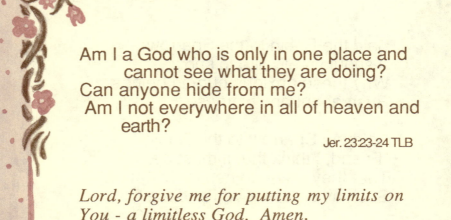

Am I a God who is only in one place and
　　　cannot see what they are doing?
Can anyone hide from me?
　Am I not everywhere in all of heaven and
　　earth?

Jer. 23:23-24 TLB

Lord, forgive me for putting my limits on
You - a limitless God. Amen.

 NOVEMBER 6

Being happy-go-lucky around a person whose heart is heavy is as bad as stealing his jacket in cold weather or rubbing salt in his wounds.

Prov. 25:20 TLB

Lord, help me to be sensitive to the needs of those around me today. Amen.

MAY 9

If anyone speaks badly of you, live so none will believe it.

A good name is more desirable than great riches.

Prov. 22:1 NIV

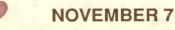

NOVEMBER 7

People don't care how much you know
until they know how much you care.

*Lord, lay some soul upon my heart and love
that soul through me. Amen.*

MAY 10

We carefully count others' offenses against us, but we rarely consider what others may suffer because of us.

T. a Kempis

It is when the Lord thinks well of a person that he is really approved and not when he thinks well of himself.

NOVEMBER 8

Every good thing the Lord had promised them came true.

Joshua 21:45 TLB

*Father, thank You that You have **always** kept Your promises. Amen.*

 MAY 11

O Lord, forever you remain the same! Your throne continues from generation to generation.

Lam. 5:19 TLB

Thank you, Father, that in this unsure, ever changing world, You are always the same. Amen.

NOVEMBER 9

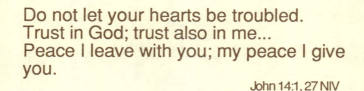

Do not let your hearts be troubled.
Trust in God; trust also in me...
Peace I leave with you; my peace I give
you.

John 14:1, 27 NIV

Thank You Father, for the promise of Your peace in the midst of all circumstances. Help me rest in it. Amen.

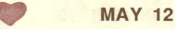

MAY 12

Thankfulness is the soil in which joy thrives.

...let us be thankful and so worship God... with reverence and awe.

Heb. 12:28 NIV

NOVEMBER 10

Never think that God's delays are God's denials.
Hold on; hold fast; hold out.
Patience is genius.

Comte de Buffon

I waited patiently for God to help me, then he listened, and heard my cry...
he lifted me...and set my feet on a hard, firm path and steadied me...
He has given me a new song to sing...

Ps. 40:1-3 TLB

MAY 13

Never confuse the will of the majority with the will of God.

Charles Colson

Do not conform any longer to the pattern of this world, but be transformed by the renewing of your mind. Then you will be able to test and approve what God's will is.

Rom. 12:2 NIV

NOVEMBER 11

Prayer is not overcoming God's reluctance;
it is laying hold of His highest willingness.

R. C. Trench

All mankind scratches for its daily bread,
but your heavenly Father knows your
needs. He will always give you all you
need from day to day if you will make the
Kingdom of God your primary concern.

Luke 12:30,31 TLB

MAY 14

God is our refuge and strength, a tested help in times of trouble. And so we need not fear even if the world blows up, and the mountains crumble into the sea.

Ps. 46:1-2 TLB

Heavenly Father, help me to live my life without giving in to the fears that surround me. Help me remembering that You hold the future! Amen.

 NOVEMBER 12

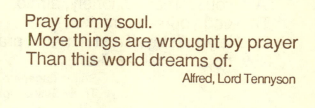

Pray for my soul.
More things are wrought by prayer
Than this world dreams of.

Alfred, Lord Tennyson

Lord, bring to my mind anyone You would have me pray for today. Amen.

MAY 15

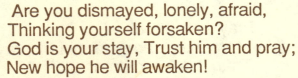

Are you dismayed, lonely, afraid,
Thinking yourself forsaken?
God is your stay, Trust him and pray;
New hope he will awaken!

Selma Lagerstrom *
Tr. E. Gustav Johnson

Lord, when doubts fill my mind, when my heart is
in turmoil, quiet me and give me renewed hope
and cheer. *Amen*..

Ps. 94:19 TLB

NOVEMBER 13

To be seventy years young is sometimes far more cheerful and hopeful than to be forty years old.

Oliver Wendell Holmes

Lord, make me more thoughtful of older people. Let me learn from their wisdom and be enriched by their experience. May I be a comfort, help and joy to them. Amen.

MAY 16

I don't mean to say I am perfect. I haven't learned all I should, but I keep working toward that day when I will finally be all that Christ saved me for and wants me to be.

Phil. 3:12 TLB

Lord, the older I get, the more I realize my need for You. Change is hard, but I desire to be more like You. Amen.

 NOVEMBER 14

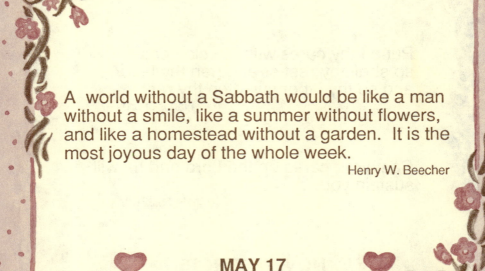

A world without a Sabbath would be like a man without a smile, like a summer without flowers, and like a homestead without a garden. It is the most joyous day of the whole week.

Henry W. Beecher

MAY 17

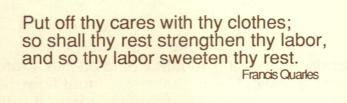

Put off thy cares with thy clothes;
so shall thy rest strengthen thy labor,
and so thy labor sweeten thy rest.

Francis Quarles

Cast your cares on the Lord and he will
sustain you.

Ps. 55:22 NIV

 NOVEMBER 15

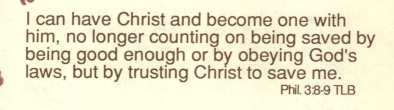

I can have Christ and become one with him, no longer counting on being saved by being good enough or by obeying God's laws, but by trusting Christ to save me.

Phil. 3:8-9 TLB

Lord, help me to trust You. It is hard to believe I don't have to perform in a set way to be acceptable to You. Help my unbelief. Amen.

MAY 18

Be very careful never to forget what you have seen God doing for you. May his miracles have a deep and permanent effect upon your lives! Tell your children and your grandchildren about the glorious miracles he did.

Deut. 4:9 TLB

All that man can do is so insignificant compared to the magnificence of Your creation. All the more, I realize my dependence on You for my smallest need. Amen.

 NOVEMBER 16

It is for us to make the effort.
The result is always in God's hands .

Mohandas K. Gandhi

We can make our plans, but the final
outcome is in God's hands.

Prov. 16:1 TLB

*Father, give me Your Holy Spirit so that my
heart will be strengthened for the work of
this day. Amen.*

 MAY 19

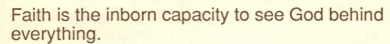

Faith is the inborn capacity to see God behind everything.

Oswald Chambers

Faith is being sure of what we hope for and certain of what we do not see.

Heb. 11:1 NIV

 NOVEMBER 17

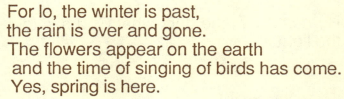

For lo, the winter is past,
the rain is over and gone.
The flowers appear on the earth
 and the time of singing of birds has come.
Yes, spring is here.

Song 2:11-12 TLB

Father, please give me ears to hear the music of the
wakening world around me. Amen.

MAY 20

Remember in the dark what God has told you in the light.

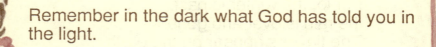

I am God, the God of your father..."Do not be afraid..."

Gen. 46:3 NIV

 NOVEMBER 18

Our Lord has written the promises of the resurrection, not in books alone, but in every leaf in Springtime.

Martin Luther

May the beauty of spring remind me of Your resurrection and of the promise of spring that is within me. Amen.

MAY 21

Most people are about as happy as they make up their minds to be.

Abraham Lincoln

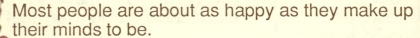

God, chase from my heart all gloomy thoughts, and make me glad with the brightness of Your hope. Amen.

 NOVEMBER 19

Words are like leaves;
And where they most abound,
much fruit of sense beneath is seldom found.

Pope

Please help me to speak freely with others, speaking with dignity, joy, and purpose. Keep me, Lord, from empty talk. Amen.

MAY 22

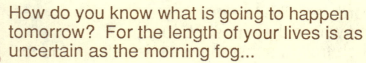

How do you know what is going to happen tomorrow? For the length of your lives is as uncertain as the morning fog...

James 4:14 TLB

Father, help me to remember that I shall pass through this life but once. Any good that I can do or any kindness that I can show, let me do it now. Amen.

NOVEMBER 20

Make two homes for thyself, my daughter. One actual home...and another spiritual home, which thou art to carry with thee always...

Catherine of Sienna

Dear Father, please make within my heart a quiet place where You will always be at home. Amen.

 MAY 23

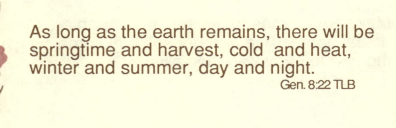

As long as the earth remains, there will be springtime and harvest, cold and heat, winter and summer, day and night.

Gen. 8:22 TLB

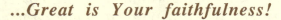

...Great is Your faithfulness!

  NOVEMBER 21

Without doubt the mightiest thought the mind can entertain is the thought of God.

A.W. Tozer

...You shall love the Lord your God with all your heart and with all your soul, and with all your mind.

Matt. 22:37 NASB

MAY 24

Worry is a thin stream of fear trickling through the mind. If encouraged, it cuts a channel into which all other thoughts are drained.

A. S. Roche

Lord, help me to release my worry and fretting to You - knowing that You hold the future and You want what is best for me.

Amen.

 NOVEMBER 22

It is said that the face is a mirror of the soul.

Lord, may Your beauty reflect through me to others. I pray that Your love will be what others see when they look at me. Amen.

MAY 25

Even if I knew that tomorrow the world
would go to pieces, I would still plant my
apple tree.

Martin Luther

And hope does not disappoint us,
because God has poured out his love into
our hearts by the Holy Spirit...

Rom. 5:5 NIV

 NOVEMBER 23

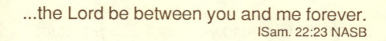

...the Lord be between you and me forever.

ISam. 22:23 NASB

Lord, I thank You for my friend. Bless and keep her, this special person You created and filled with qualities that have meant so much to me. Thank You for all the times we've shared. Bless our friendship. Amen.

MAY 26

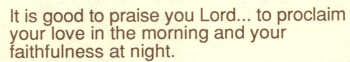

It is good to praise you Lord... to proclaim your love in the morning and your faithfulness at night.

Ps. 92:1-2 NIV

For all Your goodness, for all of life, I thank You Lord. Amen.

NOVEMBER 24

We would be more grateful if we knew how much of what we take for granted is planned by God.

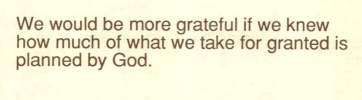

Lord, forgive me for taking so many things for granted. Thank You for caring and providing so well for me. Amen.

MAY 27

Faith is seeing a rainbow in each tear.

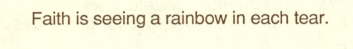

Lord when all seems dark, teach us that You are in the shadows too. Amen.

 NOVEMBER 25

When God began creating the heavens and the earth, the earth was at first a shapeless, chaotic mass... then God said, "Let there be light."

Gen. 1:1-3 TLB

Thank You Father for the reminder that You can make something wonderful out of chaos. Amen.

MAY 28

For I am convinced that nothing can ever separate us from his love. Death can't, and life can't. The angels won't, and all the powers of hell itself cannot keep God's love away.

Rom. 8:38 TLB

Knowing that I am loved by You, God, my heart is filled with thanksgiving and praise. Amen.

 NOVEMBER 26

A woman who has never seen her husband
fishing doesn't know what a patient man she
married!

A patient man has great understanding..

Prov, 14:29 NIV

MAY 29

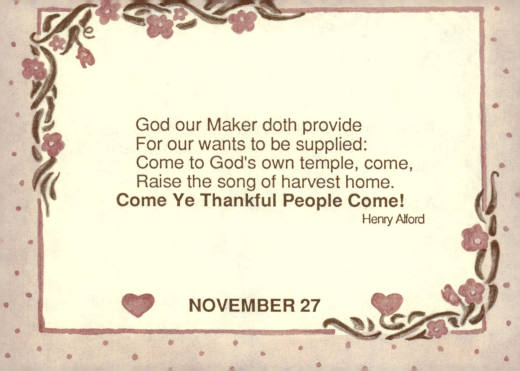

God our Maker doth provide
For our wants to be supplied:
Come to God's own temple, come,
Raise the song of harvest home.
Come Ye Thankful People Come!

Henry Alford

NOVEMBER 27

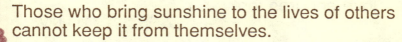

Those who bring sunshine to the lives of others cannot keep it from themselves.

James Barrie

O Lord, grant that living in Your brightness, I may bring Your sunshine into cloudy places. Amen.

MAY 30

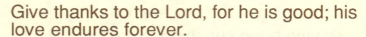

Give thanks to the Lord, for he is good; his love endures forever.

Ps. 106:1 NIV

Let us give thanks to the Lord for his unfailing love and his wonderful deeds for men.

Ps. 107:31 NIV

 NOVEMBER 28

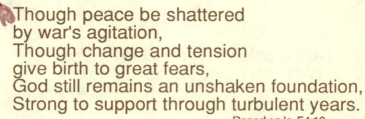

Though peace be shattered
by war's agitation,
Though change and tension
give birth to great fears,
God still remains an unshaken foundation,
Strong to support through turbulent years.

Based on Is. 54:10
Lina Sandell
Tr. Bryan Jeffrey Leech*

*Heavenly Father, when the news reports
cause anxieties and fears to surround me,
may I pause and remember that You have the
final word. Amen.*

MAY 31

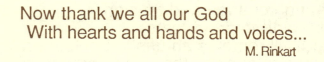

Now thank we all our God
With hearts and hands and voices...

M. Rinkart

And whatever you do, in word or deed, do
everything in the name of the Lord Jesus, giving
thanks to God the Father through him.

Col. 3:17 NASB

NOVEMBER 29

Think of no other greatness but that of the soul, no other riches but those of the heart.

John Quincy Adams

Out of his glorious, unlimited resources he will give you the mighty inner strengthening of his Holy Spirit.

Eph. 3:16 TLB

 JUNE 1

Gratitude is the memory of the heart.

You have given me so much,
please give me one thing more,
a grateful heart. Amen.

NOVEMBER 30

One cannot step twice in the same river,
for fresh waters are forever flowing
around us.

Heraclitus

*Father, keep me from the futile thoughts of
constantly reliving past experiences.
Help me to glean Your benefits from the past
and to move forward with confidence.
Amen.*

JUNE 2

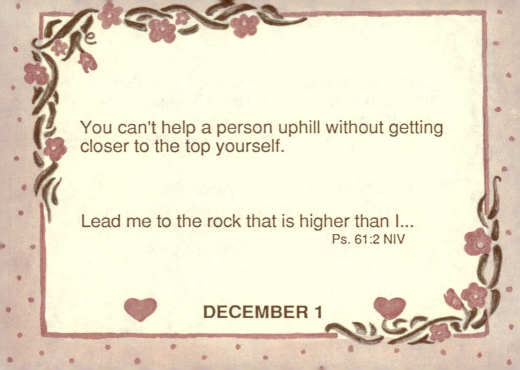

You can't help a person uphill without getting closer to the top yourself.

Lead me to the rock that is higher than I...
Ps. 61:2 NIV

DECEMBER 1

Let the honor of your neighbor be as dear to you as your own.

Lord, keep me from unkind words and unkind silences. For Christ's sake. Amen.

JUNE 3

If your troubles aren't big enough to pray about, then they certainly aren't big enough to worry and fret about.

Ask and it will be given to you...
Matt. 7:7 NIV

DECEMBER 2

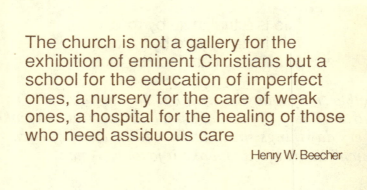

The church is not a gallery for the exhibition of eminent Christians but a school for the education of imperfect ones, a nursery for the care of weak ones, a hospital for the healing of those who need assiduous care

Henry W. Beecher

JUNE 4

Life is a trial, mile by mile.
Life is hard, yard by yard.
But it's a cinch, inch by inch.

Father, may today be exciting. Not because of extraordinary happenings but because You can make every day things special. Take full control of each "inch" in my life and make it joyous. Amen.

DECEMBER 3

Don't find fault.
Find a remedy.
Henry Ford

Father, help me be part of the solution instead of adding to the problem. Amen.

JUNE 5

But now God has shown us a different way to heaven - not by "being good enough" and trying to keep his laws, but by...coming to Christ; no matter who we are or what we have been like.

Rom. 3: 21-22 TLB

I write these things to you who believe...so that you may know that you have eternal life.

I John 5:13 NIV

 DECEMBER 4

Cheerfulness and contentment are great beautifiers and are famous preservers of youthful looks.

Charles Dickens

A cheerful look brings joy to the heart, and good news gives health to the bones.

Prov. 15:30 NIV

JUNE 6

Man has not invented God;
He has developed faith,
To meet a God already there.

Edna St. Vincent Millay

And when you draw close to God, God will draw
close to you...Let your hearts be filled with God
alone...

James 4:8 TLB

DECEMBER 5

The only people to get even with
are those who have helped you!

May God who gives patience, steadiness
and encouragement help you to live in
complete harmony with each other - each
with the attitude of Christ toward the other.

Rom. 15:5 TLB

JUNE 7

...though I fall I will rise again! When I sit in darkness, the Lord himself will be my Light.

Micah 7:8 TLB

Jesus said, "I am the light of the world. Whoever follows me will never walk in darkness, but will have the light of life."

John 8:12 NIV

DECEMBER 6

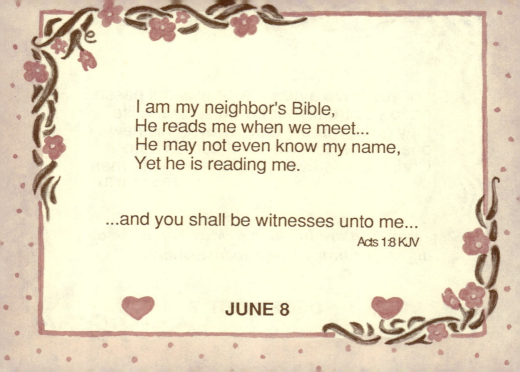

I am my neighbor's Bible,
He reads me when we meet...
He may not even know my name,
Yet he is reading me.

...and you shall be witnesses unto me...

Acts 1:8 KJV

JUNE 8

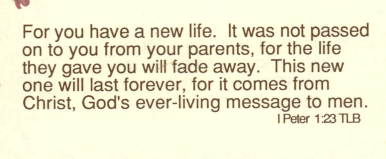

For you have a new life. It was not passed on to you from your parents, for the life they gave you will fade away. This new one will last forever, for it comes from Christ, God's ever-living message to men.

I Peter 1:23 TLB

Jesus, You are life to me. May You make a difference in my living today. Amen.

DECEMBER 7

The entire law is summed up in a single command:

"Love your neighbor as yourself."

Gal. 5:14 NIV

But Lord, it's so hard sometimes!
Please give me Your love - in Jesus' name.
Amen.

JUNE 9

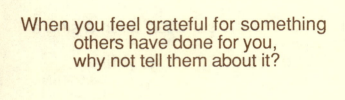

When you feel grateful for something
others have done for you,
why not tell them about it?

*Don't let me get so busy that I forget to show
gratefulness to others. Help me to especially
appreciate the loved ones You have given to
me. Amen.*

  DECEMBER 8

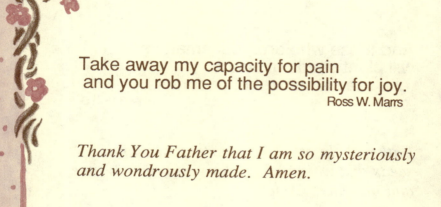

Take away my capacity for pain
and you rob me of the possibility for joy.

Ross W. Marrs

*Thank You Father that I am so mysteriously
and wondrously made. Amen.*

JUNE 10

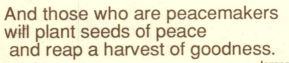

And those who are peacemakers
will plant seeds of peace
and reap a harvest of goodness.

James 3:18 TLB

*Father, help me to remember that planting
seeds and waiting for a harvest requires time
and patience. Amen.*

DECEMBER 9

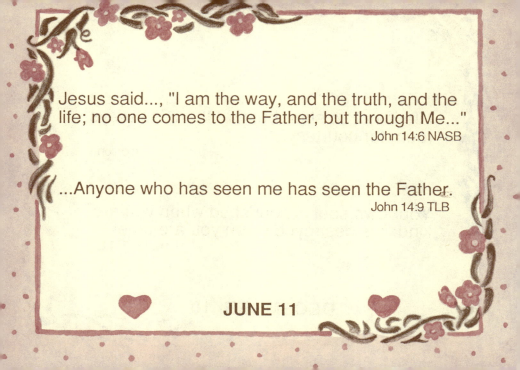

Jesus said..., "I am the way, and the truth, and the life; no one comes to the Father, but through Me..."

John 14:6 NASB

...Anyone who has seen me has seen the Father.

John 14:9 TLB

JUNE 11

Life is not so short but that there is always room for courtesy.

Emerson

Your own soul is nourished when you are kind; it is destroyed when you are cruel.

Prov. 11:17 TLB

 DECEMBER 10

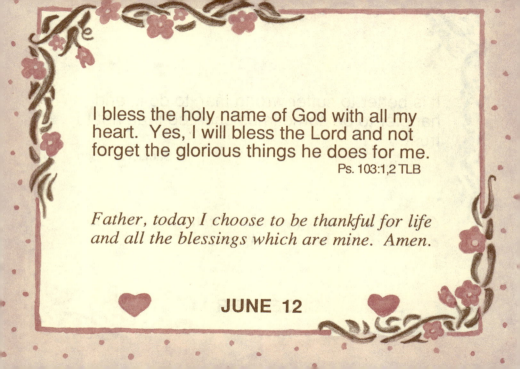

I bless the holy name of God with all my heart. Yes, I will bless the Lord and not forget the glorious things he does for me.

Ps. 103:1,2 TLB

Father, today I choose to be thankful for life and all the blessings which are mine. Amen.

JUNE 12

It is better to suffer wrong than to do it, and happier to be sometimes cheated than not to trust.

Samuel Johnson

Give me a trusting heart Lord and the wisdom to depend only upon You. Amen.

 DECEMBER 11

The gem cannot be polished without friction
Nor the child of God perfected without adversity.

*Heavenly Father, help me not to resist Your desired
changes within me. Continue to polish me. Amen.*

JUNE 13

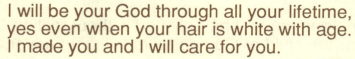

I will be your God through all your lifetime,
yes even when your hair is white with age.
I made you and I will care for you.

Is. 46:4 TLB

Surely goodness and lovingkindness will
follow me all the days of my life, and I will
dwell in the house of the Lord forever.

Ps. 23:6 NASB

 DECEMBER 12

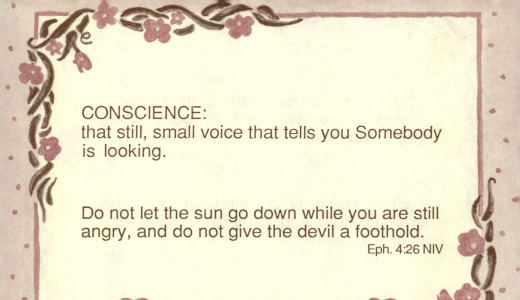

CONSCIENCE:
that still, small voice that tells you Somebody
is looking.

Do not let the sun go down while you are still
angry, and do not give the devil a foothold.

Eph. 4:26 NIV

JUNE 14

I have been driven many times to my
knees by the overwhelming conviction
that I had nowhere else to go.

Abraham Lincoln

...when you pray, go into your room and
shut the door and pray to your Father
who is in secret...

Matt. 6:6 RSV

 DECEMBER 13

For knowledge to become wisdom
and for the soul to grow, the soul must be
rooted in God.

Mountford

Let your roots grow down deeply in him
and draw up nourishment from him.
See that you go on growing in the Lord,
and become strong and vigorous in the
truth you were taught...

Col 2:7 TLB

JUNE 15

...I am sure that God who began the good work within you will keep right on helping you grow in his grace until this task within you is finally finished on that day when Jesus Christ returns.

Phil. 1:6 TLB

Lord, sometimes my progress seems so slow. Thank You for Your faithfulness and perseverance. Help me to keep sight of the "finished task". Amen.

 DECEMBER 14

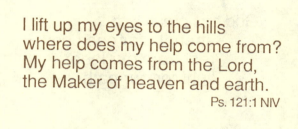

I lift up my eyes to the hills
where does my help come from?
My help comes from the Lord,
the Maker of heaven and earth.

Ps. 121:1 NIV

Thank You Lord for reminding me that You are the source of my strength. Amen.

JUNE 16

God has promised:
-strength for each day
-rest from our labor
-light for our path.

Light of the world, let Your light be the center of our Christmas activities. Amen.

DECEMBER 15

God made you as you are
in order to use you as He planned.
S.C. McAuley

Father, help me appreciate who I am in Your sight and give me the desire to be used by You. Amen.

 JUNE 17

If I can stop one heart from breaking, I shall not live in vain.

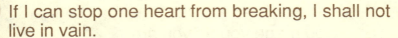

Emily Dickinson

Father, give me Your heart and use me to reach out to someone in need. To some, this season brings much loneliness and pain. Lead me to the ones who need to experience the joy of Your companionship. Amen.

DECEMBER 16

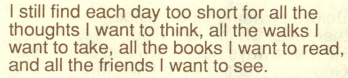

I still find each day too short for all the thoughts I want to think, all the walks I want to take, all the books I want to read, and all the friends I want to see.

John Burroughs

Lord, help me to use the time You've given to me wisely. Thank You for life and for all that is available to me. Amen.

JUNE 18

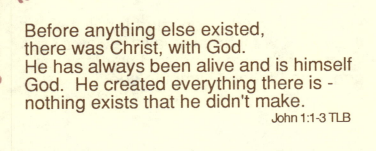

Before anything else existed,
there was Christ, with God.
He has always been alive and is himself
God. He created everything there is -
nothing exists that he didn't make.

John 1:1-3 TLB

You, Lord Jesus, are the Supreme Authority;
my soul praises You. Amen.

DECEMBER 17

This is too glorious, too wonderful to believe! I can never be lost to your Spirit! I can never get away from my God!

Ps. 139:6-7 TLB

...wherever I am, You are there - that is truly good news! Amen.

JUNE 19

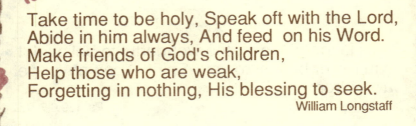

Take time to be holy, Speak oft with the Lord,
Abide in him always, And feed on his Word.
Make friends of God's children,
Help those who are weak,
Forgetting in nothing, His blessing to seek.

William Longstaff

*Father, You are with me constantly - help me
to find special times to rest in Your presence.
Daily I need to take time to be holy. Amen.*

DECEMBER 18

Learn to say kind things -
nobody ever resents them -

Heavenly Father, it's easy to fall into the bad habit of saying whatever I please. Give me the love and kindness of Jesus. Amen.

JUNE 20

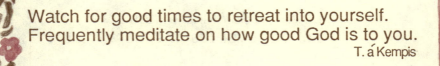

Watch for good times to retreat into yourself.
Frequently meditate on how good God is to you.

T. á Kempis

*Lord, help me find time to focus on You - the reason
for this wonderful season. Amen.*

DECEMBER 19

It's good to have money and the things that money can buy, but it's good, too, to check up once in a while and make sure you haven't lost the things that money can't buy.

G. H. Larimer

..."Beware that in your plenty you don't forget the Lord your God and begin to disobey him."

Deut. 8:11 TLB

JUNE 21

Never lose sight of the fact that old age needs so little but needs that little so much.

Margaret Willour

...love one another. As I have loved you so you must love one another.

John 13:34 NIV

 DECEMBER 20

The true calling of a Christian is not to do extraordinary things but to do ordinary things in an extraordinary way.

Dean Stanley

Father, help me to not tire of doing the ordinary things in life. Help me season each task with Your love and grace. In Jesus' name. Amen.

 **JUNE 22**

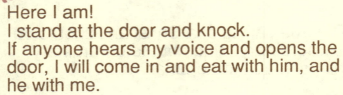

Here I am!
I stand at the door and knock.
If anyone hears my voice and opens the
door, I will come in and eat with him, and
he with me.

Rev. 3:20 NIV

I open the door of my heart now Lord, so
that You may come in and dwell in me.
Thank You for the assurance of my salvation
through Christ. Amen.

 DECEMBER 21

You alone are the Lord.
You made the heavens...
and all their starry host,
the earth and all that is on it,
the seas and all that is in them.
You give life to everything,
and the multitudes of heaven worship you.

Neh. 9:6 NIV

JUNE 23

...Fix your thoughts on what is true and good and right...

Think about things that are pure and lovely, and dwell on the fine, good things in others.

Think about all you can praise God for and be glad about.

Phil 4:8 TLB

When counting my blessings I hardly know where to begin! Give me a thankful heart this day. Amen.

DECEMBER 22

If I were to be described in one word, what would it be?

Lord, direct me today as I ponder this question. Amen.

JUNE 24

And Christ became a human being
and lived here on earth among us
and was full of loving forgiveness
and truth.

John 1:14 TLB

*Father, thank You for coming to earth to be
my Savior. Amen.*

 DECEMBER 23

The tiniest dewdrop hanging from a grass blade in the morning is big enough to reflect the sunshine and the blue of the sky.

Lord, I pray that I will reflect Your love today. Amen.

JUNE 25

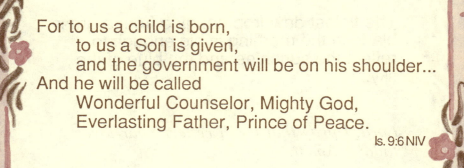

For to us a child is born,
    to us a Son is given,
    and the government will be on his shoulder...
And he will be called
    Wonderful Counselor, Mighty God,
    Everlasting Father, Prince of Peace.

Is. 9:6 NIV

DECEMBER 24

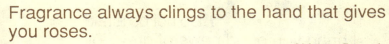

Fragrance always clings to the hand that gives
you roses.

Chinese Proverb

Your own soul is nourished when you are kind;
it is destroyed when you are cruel.

Prov. 11:17 TLB

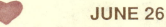

JUNE 26

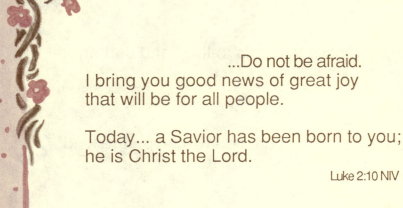

...Do not be afraid.
I bring you good news of great joy
that will be for all people.

Today... a Savior has been born to you;
he is Christ the Lord.

Luke 2:10 NIV

 **DECEMBER 25**

May you always be doing those good kind things which show that you are a child of God, for this will bring much praise and glory to God.

Phil. 1:11 TLB

Father, give me the energy and the strength to do what You would have me do. Help me to find time for everything that is important to You. Amen.

 JUNE 27

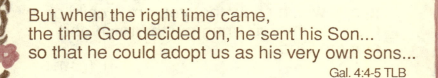

But when the right time came,
the time God decided on, he sent his Son...
so that he could adopt us as his very own sons...

Gal. 4:4-5 TLB

...Thanks be to God for his unspeakable gift!

II Cor. 9:15 KJV

DECEMBER 26

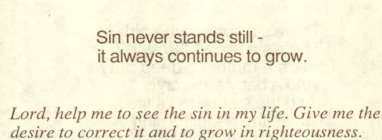

Sin never stands still -
it always continues to grow.

*Lord, help me to see the sin in my life. Give me the
desire to correct it and to grow in righteousness.
Amen.*

JUNE 28

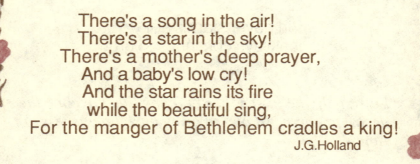

There's a song in the air!
There's a star in the sky!
There's a mother's deep prayer,
And a baby's low cry!
And the star rains its fire
while the beautiful sing,
For the manger of Bethlehem cradles a king!

J.G.Holland

DECEMBER 27

Gentle words cause life and health;
griping brings discouragement.

Prov. 15:4 TLB

*Lord, help me to always speak gentle, life-giving
words. Amen.*

JUNE 29

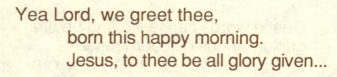

Yea Lord, we greet thee,
　　 born this happy morning.
　　　 Jesus, to thee be all glory given...

F. Oakeley

Father, remind me again this Christmas and throughout the year of the miracle of Your love. Amen.

 DECEMBER 28

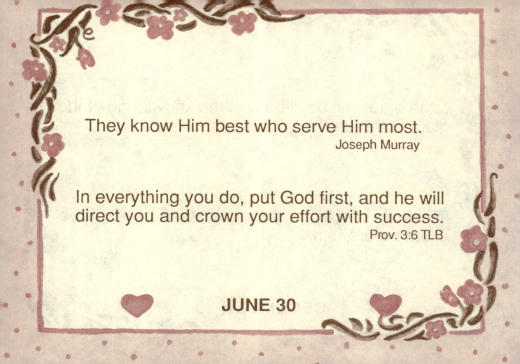

They know Him best who serve Him most.

Joseph Murray

In everything you do, put God first, and he will direct you and crown your effort with success.

Prov. 3:6 TLB

JUNE 30

...the earth will be filled with the knowledge of the glory of the Lord...

Hab. 2:14 NIV

The Lord is in his holy temple; let all the earth be silent before him.

Hab. 2:20 NIV

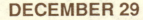 **DECEMBER 29**

If you would lift me,
you must be on higher ground.

Emerson

Lord, keep me eager to seek Thy will and to follow Thee. Lift me up to higher ground. Amen.

JULY 1

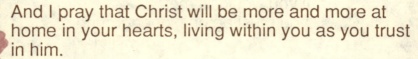

And I pray that Christ will be more and more at home in your hearts, living within you as you trust in him.

Eph. 3:7 TLB

Lord, this is my earnest prayer as I look toward a new year with You. Amen.

DECEMBER 30

Please turn the book over and begin again for July through December.

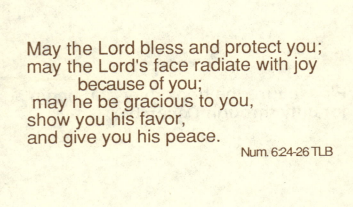

May the Lord bless and protect you;
may the Lord's face radiate with joy
because of you;
may he be gracious to you,
show you his favor,
and give you his peace.

Num. 6:24-26 TLB

DECEMBER 31

REORDER FORM

Quantity	Product	Price	Total
	Bless Your Heart (gift edition)	$14.95	
	Bless Your Heart (men's edition)	$14.95	
		Total	

Shipping and Handling included in price

☐ Check enclosed for total amount (make check payable to Samplers)

☐ Charge my **MasterCard** ☐ Master Card **VISA** ☐ VISA

Account No.

Mail reorder form to:
Samplers
9947 Valley View Road
Minneapolis, MN 55344

612-942-7754

☐☐☐☐ ☐☐☐☐ ☐☐☐☐ ☐☐☐☐

Expiration Date: Month_____ Year_____

Signature _____
(required on all charge orders)

Ship to: Name _____

Street _____

City _____ State _____ Zip _____